Marcus Smith has a PhD from the Australian National University and a master's degree from the University of Cambridge. He is an associate professor in law at Charles Sturt University where he researches and teaches technology law and regulation. He has published a wide range of books and articles on the subject, and has delivered presentations around the world, including in China, India, Europe, the United States and the United Kingdom. He previously worked in legal, policy and research positions for the Australian government.

TECHNO

MARCUS SMITH

UQP

First published 2024 by University of Queensland Press
PO Box 6042, St Lucia, Queensland 4067 Australia

University of Queensland Press (UQP) acknowledges the Traditional Owners and their custodianship of the lands on which UQP operates. We pay our respects to their Ancestors and their descendants, who continue cultural and spiritual connections to Country. We recognise their valuable contributions to Australian and global society.

uqp.com.au
reception@uqp.com.au

Cover design by Luke Causby, Blue Cork
Author image supplied by https://thorsonphotography.com.au/contact/
Typeset in 12/17 pt Bembo Std by Post Pre-press Group, Brisbane
Printed in Australia by McPherson's Printing Group

University of Queensland Press is assisted by the Australian Government through Creative Australia, its principal arts investment and advisory body.

A catalogue record for this book is available from the National Library of Australia.

ISBN 978 0 7022 6641 6 (pbk)
ISBN 978 0 7022 6936 3 (epdf)
ISBN 978 0 7022 6937 0 (epub)

University of Queensland Press uses papers that are natural, renewable and recyclable products made from wood grown in well-managed forests and other controlled sources. The logging and manufacturing processes conform to the environmental regulations of the country of origin.

techno

/ˈtek.nəʊ /

adj. relating to or involving technology:
the techno revolution.

CONTENTS

Preface

Our Creation

We are living in the midst of a technology revolution and the rise of artificial intelligence (AI). New technologies are continually being created; we are encouraged to enjoy their benefits and not think too much about the wider implications. Smartphones, social media, biometrics and renewable energy are all part of an explosion of new technology, and at the centre of it all is AI.

We all use technology, and it has changed our daily lives in many positive ways. But has there been enough effort devoted to considering the costs and how they can be addressed? Costs like data theft and privacy breaches, loss of autonomy and individual rights, technology-enabled abuse, fraud, social inequality and workforce impacts. This book is about the way technology is adopted, how it is influencing government, individuals and society, and its implications. It looks at the relationship between humans and technology, and considers how that is affecting us and what we can do about it.

The present moment is a critical time in the development of new technologies. A growing number of people are beginning to question whether we are creating things we cannot control. The prospect that technology may even lead to the end of human civilisation is now being taken seriously. On the horizon is the need to address the issue of 'artificial general intelligence' (AGI), when technology will exceed human intelligence and have the capacity to evolve and improve itself.

Human creation of advanced technologies, such as AI, evokes imagery from the great art of the Renaissance. In Michelangelo's fresco of the creation narrative from the Book of Genesis, God is depicted giving life to Adam through his outstretched finger; humans are created in God's image and likeness. God also creates Eve, and places her and Adam in the Garden of Eden to enjoy an exotic paradise of plants and animals.

Adam and Eve could eat from any tree in the Garden of Eden, except for the 'tree of knowledge'. Alas, a serpent seduced Eve into eating the forbidden fruit:

> 'You will not certainly die,' the serpent said to the woman. 'For God knows that when you eat from it your eyes will be opened, and you will be like God, knowing good and evil.'[1]

Desiring wisdom, Adam and Eve both eat the fruit, and as punishment are expelled from paradise. They sought knowledge and control of the world, just as we humans continue to do today. Is the creation of increasingly complex technologies our great temptation? And, if we don't retain control of them, will they eventually cost us our paradise?

A quarter of the way through the twenty-first century, human creations, advancements in technologies such as AI and genomics offer us tempting powers to reshape ourselves and the world in ways that have never before been possible. AI is especially significant, as it can be integrated with other technologies, enhancing their potency, efficiency and impact. We must begin to appreciate the potential for technology to quietly evolve beyond the power of humans to control it.

AI is at the forefront of a cluster of sophisticated technologies that have emerged over the past twenty-five years. It is not since atomic weapons were developed that technology has been spoken about in these terms. But we are coming to understand that AI does potentially have similar implications. Technology can enhance our living standards, but its benefits may come at an incalculable cost. Unlike nuclear weapons, the risk isn't that one country will use it against another – although that is a possibility; it is that the technology itself may one day overcome humans, and we may be powerless to compete, unless careful, well-thought-out regulation is put in place to control how it can be developed and used. Contemporary technology is complex, rapidly evolving and has worldwide implications – and it is not just AI we should be concerned about.

While adopting new technologies is not itself an issue, lack of regulation can become a significant problem. The extent to which governments have effectively controlled new technologies is limited – where they have done anything at all. Many technologies are sold and used globally; national governments have not sufficiently applied themselves to this important task.

We should be optimistic that the necessary regulation is possible, and we should continue to work towards it. Once we can regulate appropriately and adapt to this technology revolution, humans and technology can coexist harmoniously, and to our significant benefit. But we need a greater focus on limiting the costs, not just on harnessing the positives. This book documents our present era of technology *revolution* and aims to prepare us for the next one, which must be characterised by effective technology *regulation*. It is critical that we understand what these technologies are, how they can be used and what we can do to control them.

Technology *revolution* refers to the present era, in which many fields of technology are changing human life at a rapid pace. How we generate electricity, how we use data, how governments enforce the law, how we are identified, how we communicate, our healthcare, and how we live, work and transact with one another have all undergone remarkable change in a relatively short period of time. The next chapter will discuss this concept in more detail, and consider the way this revolution defines the period in history we are living through.

Technology *regulation* must be a corollary of the technology revolution. It refers to the next era, in which we will appropriately and continually address the current issues that have arisen, like how to reduce the likelihood that new technology will harm us, how we protect against impacts on the environment, how we plan for the changes to society it brings, how we maintain fundamental rights such as privacy, and how we uphold fairness, democratic institutions and free markets. While technology regulation is discussed throughout the entire book, the final chapter is dedicated to it and highlights some key components.

The relationship between humans and technology is the most vital and pressing social, political and ethical issue of our lifetime. It is not just the domain of politicians, technology entrepreneurs and scientists – it affects us all. We need to understand and appreciate the implications of technology. We need to engage with these issues, despite their challenges, and to think about how governments should act to implement effective technology regulation: that is the focus of this book.

1. Techno

Technology Revolution

The progressive development of technology has always been an important human endeavour. We can all observe how new technology is changing our lives. Changing them in small, incremental ways – a slimmer phone with more features, a new app – and in bigger ways, such as the transition from combustion engines to electric vehicles. It has been suggested that we may be sleepwalking into a catastrophe in the way we are adopting new technology, not thinking hard enough about the potential negative consequences.[1]

New technology has revolutionised humans' capacity to influence the world. Using our intellects to create things and then applying them to improve our lives are central traits that define us. The ability to commercialise a new technology is the most richly rewarded of human activities. The wealthiest individuals in the world today became so not by inventing the technology that underlies their business, but by applying it in a way that creates value, giving people something they want ... or think they need.

Whether with smartphones, online platforms, management software, diagnostic tools or electric cars, technology companies have created new industries and led this technology revolution. Their leaders' ideas and products have transformed us, become part of our lives, shaped our interactions and guided our personal and professional progress, influencing the way we perceive and interact with the world, as well as how we interpret it.

You probably know this already. What you may not have thought as much about is why we need to control these revolutionary technologies. Too many of us are simply living in the moment, marvelling at the efficiency, convenience and size of new technologies, and adopting them as soon as they become available. But it is increasingly important for governments, societies and individuals to think about regulating technology. It is important for humanity.

New laws and regulation necessarily come after a technology has been developed, and after its function, operation and potential are understood (or thought to be understood). But although the question of regulation comes second, it is not secondary. As technology capabilities, automation, AI and machine-learning techniques grow in sophistication with each passing year, questions about how they should be used grow in importance. Understanding not only the technology and the people behind it but also how it should be controlled, regulated and governed is vital. The technology revolution has driven the recent history of the world, and will shape the future.

The technology revolution follows earlier revolutions of the steam engine, electricity and computing. The present one is driven by online networks, wi-fi, data analytics and AI. We have progressed from the computer revolution of the 1980s and 1990s into a technology revolution centred on data and automation. This one may have greater implications for human beings than any previous. Key to it all is the growing capacity of AI technology to use data and algorithms autonomously – to think for humans, to think and grow faster than humans can, to think beyond humans, and potentially, through AGI, to evolve independently of humans. This revolution is not happening only in the technology industry, but in healthcare, business, government administration, law enforcement, professional services, warfare and education – it permeates all aspects of human society.

During the earlier revolutions, the separation between humans and the technology we invented was more distinct than it is today. When a human operated a steam engine or used an electrical appliance, there was a clearer delineation between person and machine. This narrowed with the advent of computers. They started to become an extension of the brain, being programmed to do calculations and other types of work that a human mind could not do as efficiently, and to create more abstract outputs and products. The delineation is narrowing again during the present technological revolution.

When we use social media or biometric authentication, the separation between ourselves and the data about ourselves is even less distinct. This is a trend that will continue.

Personal computers were developed forty years ago, and they continue to become more advanced in their complexity and capabilities. But what will computers be like in the next quarter of a century? And what kind of society will we live in? By then, today's technology will seem as basic to us as the computers of twenty-five years ago appear now. The world will have changed, and humans' place within it will have shifted. The AI of today offers only a glimpse of what society will look like in the 2050s. By then, computers will invent and innovate far more autonomously. Intelligent machines will be making everyday decisions for humans, thinking and working for us. If they advance to reach the inflection point known as AGI, it will be a momentous and daunting moment in human history.

This 'singularity', when AI can think and evolve independently of humans, is still some way off – and theoretical – but we should consider it now. There will be great benefits for humanity if technology can be equitably distributed across the world, and regulated effectively. Science and technology should not be exploited by the wealthiest individuals or countries. We are all impacted by technology. Controlling these technologies will be no easy task. We must understand them, the companies that make them, the issues they raise and the governments that utilise and regulate them.

∞

Technology revolution and regulation affects everyone, all over the world. To understand it, we need a variety of perspectives from different countries. In this book, we look at examples from the United States, China, Australia and Europe.

The United States is an amazing country, spanning vast landscapes, from the sprawling metropolis of New York City, the deserts of Arizona, the beaches of California, the mountains of Colorado and the Florida Keys. Globally, it remains the most important country in technology investment, innovation and influence. It has been the dominant world power for more than a century across many fields, driven by knowledge, technology and business.

Almost all of the world's leading tech companies were founded in the United States. Their leaders and employees were educated there. It is the market where they were formed and grew, before expanding across the globe. During the industrial revolution there was Edison and Ford; during the first technology revolution there was Gates and Jobs; and today there is Musk and Bezos. The United States is the birthplace of space exploration, the personal computer, the internet, search engines, social media networks, smartphones and electric cars.

A capitalist liberal democracy, with freedoms enshrined in its constitution and bill of rights, the United States is perhaps also the dominant culture in the world today. Its food, films, brands, actors, sport stars, entrepreneurs and technology companies influence billions of people. It prides itself on its free-market capitalism – on being a country where anyone can make it to the top. If the American dream is becoming 'rich and famous', then many of those exemplifying it are the tech entrepreneurs.

Its technology companies – such as Tesla, Meta, Uber, Amazon, Apple and Alphabet – lead the technological revolution. The founders who have driven these companies forward, amassing unprecedented levels of wealth and influence, are admired for their intellect and vision, but are also criticised for their data acquisition, dominance and monopolisation of markets.

These gifted intellects – creative physicists, engineers and computer scientists – hold the skills most highly valued in today's economy, and they continue to be admired internationally for their foresight and vision. The platforms they have created – YouTube, eBay, Facebook, X (formerly Twitter), Instagram, Ethereum and Google, among others – have been embraced, not only as platforms for sharing information, but as a means for many to make money, providing broader access to markets than was possible in previous generations. They have driven the economic shift away from bricks-and-mortar sales to online commerce. They have opened up new ways of building wealth.

Most books on new technology look at the issue from a US perspective, as that is where most of it has been developed. But to best appreciate the technology revolution today, a global perspective is needed. While the United States will remain central, there will be geopolitical change over the next twenty-five years. China, in particular, is likely to rival the United States, and although it has been less innovative in developing new technologies to date, it has the expertise, knowledge, resources and scale to become the world leader and dominant superpower.

∞

With 1.5 billion people, China has almost five times the population of the United States. It is the world's second-largest economy today, and the fastest growing. It is known as the factory of the world, producing steel, chemicals, clothing and electronics – including smartphones, laptops, watches and televisions – and, increasingly, semiconductors, despite trade sanctions.[2] Economically, China has become more capitalist. Its citizens and government consume a great deal of technology, and it now has its own major technology companies that are expanding to global markets. Its integration of technology into government administration, particularly in its use of automated identification and processing within its social credit system, is especially interesting, providing an insight into future governance around the world.

Examining the recent history of technology without considering China would be an oversight. While technology companies and cultural icons from the United States are still dominating the world, China is becoming more innovative in developing technology of its own, particularly in the areas of finance, biotechnology, surveillance, autonomous weapons and space technology. And with many more engineering graduates annually in China compared with the United States, it already has a greater number of people working in technology fields and is rapidly gaining expertise.[3] China's technological advancement is a key factor in present geopolitical developments, and has contributed significantly to its economic and military expansion, and its growth in global influence.

China is well placed to capitalise on the coming technological revolution. Data will become increasingly central to government and business in the twenty-first century, to an even greater extent than it is already, and with 1.5 billion citizens it has a lot of it. While the Chinese social credit system is criticised in the West as emblematic of an authoritarian government, similar systems are already being used in liberal democracies too: biometric facial recognition at passport control, public CCTV, metadata retention and online administration systems. The technology revolution is intertwined with the contemporary global economic and political landscape. China is rapidly expanding its assets and capabilities, modernising its armed forces and apparently leading the United States in developing new military capabilities such as hypersonic weapons. In response, the United States is expanding its relationships with Australia, Japan and India, forming the Quad group, as well as AUKUS with Australia and the United Kingdom, focused on sharing military technology and assets.[4]

∞

While the United States and China remain the most significant rivals in this technology revolution, there are smaller countries wedged between them that will play an important role. With its economic links to China and its defence links to the United States, Australia has an interesting perspective. It is a major consumer of technology. In fact, Australia is one of the wealthiest and most advanced economies in the world, despite its small population of only 26 million. To properly understand the impact of technology and how it is best regulated, we need these further perspectives. Australia can regulate from a more objective standpoint, not being home to the large technology companies, and therefore not having as much to lose when seeking to control them.

When you think of Australia, the first thing that comes to mind is likely not sophisticated technology or innovative regulatory approaches. For many people, it's Australia's beautiful natural environment and wildlife. Despite its somewhat isolated location, it actually has the world's highest median wealth and living standards, on a par with those of Switzerland and Scandinavia. Australia's developed economy was built on the exporting of resources, which has funded its high living standards – and created a high cost of living, including some of the world's most expensive real estate.

Australia has vast natural resources, and exports huge amounts of iron ore from the Pilbara, in the country's west, to China. The large continent is also well placed to transition into a major provider of renewable energy, such as solar, wind and hydro. It already provides three-quarters of Tesla's lithium, and more than a third of its nickel, both vital components of electric vehicle batteries.[5] Traditionally, it has not been especially innovative, and has certainly not created a great deal of technology that has influenced the world in the way that the United States, China, Japan or Germany has done. But it has made a few significant contributions, such as the research that led to wi-fi and the cochlear implant.[6] Although its technology sector is far behind that of the United States by any measure, it does have some large software companies, including Atlassian and Canva.

For anyone thinking about future technology regulation globally, Australia should be kept in mind. As will be discussed later, Australian politicians are pushing back and regulating the United States' technology companies that have brought their platforms down under, with some interesting results. Whether it is the geographical isolation of the country, the system of government or something about the Australian mindset, its politicians have managed to achieve some regulatory outcomes that liberal-democratic governments in the United Kingdom, Scandinavia, Canada and elsewhere couldn't. They have forced these companies to change their policies in key areas in which they clashed with the national interest, although this is a battle that will continue. In some cases, once this was achieved in Australia, other countries have followed suit – Canada, the United Kingdom, the United States – and the power of the companies to dictate government policy has begun to wane. Australian is now punching above its weight in technology regulation, introducing world-first laws in fields like social media and the application of law-enforcement technologies.

∞

Last but certainly not least, especially from the perspective of regulating US technology companies, is Europe. Its name is thought to derive from a combination of the Greek word roots *eur* (wide) and *op* (see), and so may mean 'wide-gazing'. The continent has a rich cultural history, so much so that it is sometimes described as the birthplace of Western civilisation.[7] The continent has great linguistic diversity among its many countries. Its contribution to cultural fields, including music, art, philosophy, food, architecture and design, has been immense. Ancient Greece is associated with the development of the concept of democracy, shifting away from a hereditary ruler to a political body that represents citizens.

In the twentieth century, the two world wars reshaped the continent, and European leadership in world politics was diminished. Today, the European Union has twenty-seven member states, which have committed to maintaining a democratically elected government, a free-market economy and the rule of law. But there are complexities associated with such a broad union. Following the global financial crisis in 2008, there has been ongoing tension between the financially stable countries and those that are indebted. And of course there was Brexit in 2020, in which the people of the United Kingdom elected to leave the European Union. More positively, the European Union is a fine example of intergovernmental collaboration, and has achieved progressive laws and policies on climate change and technology regulation.[8]

In the area of technology policy, the General Data Protection Regulation, introduced in 2018, improved the security of EU citizens' data following the rise of the internet and online business. It also applies to companies based beyond European shores that hold the data of EU citizens. In this way, it has shaped technology policy worldwide. Europe continues to take a strong stance against the large tech companies, such as Meta, Alphabet, Apple and Microsoft, issuing big fines for anti-competitive behaviour and data-protection issues. It is establishing the world's first regulatory regime for AI.[9]

∞

Over the past twenty-five years, humans have been developing, improving and commercialising new technologies at scale, applying scientific research and data analytics to achieve tasks more quickly, autonomously and efficiently, and at lower cost. Capabilities like automation, artificial intelligence and machine learning grow in sophistication with each passing year, but so do questions about how they should be used.

So much of what humanity does is reliant on technology, but comparatively little time and effort is devoted to the vital activity of technology regulation, a task that is difficult in a globalised world that is changing so rapidly.

As well as looking at technological innovations from political, commercial and rights-based perspectives, we need to understand the basics of how they work, where they're being used and what their implications are. We should be proactive in understanding their costs and benefits. They will affect all of us, and a better understanding of these issues is the first step towards improving how we respond to them. We need to define what is acceptable to us and to what extent we are willing to trade off individual rights, such as privacy and autonomy, in order to enjoy the benefits of these new technologies.

How are humans going to coexist with technology as it becomes even more sophisticated, and where should the distinction between humans and technology be drawn?

This book is divided into three parts, focusing on government, the individual and society. For governments, technology presents a range of challenges, relating to artificial intelligence, to the resources associated with renewable technology and to shifting geopolitical power dynamics. We will explore how the administration of society is becoming automated, with data and software increasingly used to manage access to services.

In the context of individuals, we discuss the relationship between people and their data through technologies like smartphones, biometric identification and genomics. Smartphone metadata is becoming a proxy for activity, and biometrics a proxy for identity. We look at how this data can be used by companies, governments and law enforcement, and how it forms the basis of systems that use it to regulate individuals. Other forms of data are becoming important too. Genomic data is increasingly being utilised to inform individual health diagnostics and treatment, and could be used for other public health and identification purposes by companies and governments.

At the level of society, we will look at how social interactions have largely moved online, facilitated by platforms like Facebook. Deregulated transactions within societies can now be facilitated by Bitcoin, Ether and smart contracts. We will also look at the ongoing attempts by governments and courts to control the internet and multinational online businesses that have had mixed success.

This book is about the technology revolution: how it is changing the world and what we need to do about that. We are approaching a critical point. If AI and other new technologies continue to be implemented rapidly without a focus on controlling risks and developing necessary laws, there will be a catastrophe: we need better technology regulation.

PART 1

TECHNOLOGY AND GOVERNMENT

Governments dictate the relationship between humans and technology by defining whether it can be used, how it can be used, and the extent to which it is controlled. In any government, there is usually a parliament to make laws, a court system, and a means of administering and enforcing law through police and the civil service. Governments fall on a spectrum, ranging from democracies, where authority is delegated to public officials that the community elects; to totalitarianism, where one political party dictates laws and has no opposition; with authoritarianism falling somewhere in between.

The issues in relation to technology and government reflect those that arise in relation to societies and individuals, we are just looking at them from a broader perspective. Governments need to consider the underlying factors and wider implications associated with new technologies. The questions here are big: how to deal with artificial intelligence; the internet; renewable technology; critical minerals supply; globalisation; geopolitics and military conflict. Will governments be able to respond effectively in the future as technology and AI becomes even more sophisticated?

The discussion of technology and government is related to the issue of technology regulation, which we return to throughout, but especially in the final chapter of the book. The most vital and complex question at the heart of the interaction of humans and technology is: how can governments regulate technology effectively?

2. Means of Production

Critical Resources

China has been building military infrastructure on the Spratly Islands, in the South China Sea, since 2013. Disputes over maritime boundaries among countries in the region have been widely reported. They involve Taiwan, Indonesia, Malaysia, Vietnam, Brunei and the Philippines, and relate to boundaries, reefs and island chains. Further complicating this situation is the issue China has with Taiwan over the latter's status. Although Taiwan has been governed independently since 1949, the government of the People's Republic of China views it as part of its territory. Indeed, China has the stated goal of unifying Taiwan with the mainland, using military force if necessary.[1]

There are several reasons why this part of the world is strategically important. Over 500 million people live around the coastline of the South China Sea. There are the trade routes: each year, a third of global maritime trade, valued at over US$3 trillion, passes through this sea, including around 40 per cent of China's trade. The shipping lanes are therefore globally significant. Beyond that, the area is rich in natural resources, such as fish stocks, natural gas and crude oil. It has been estimated that it contains more than 11 billion barrels of oil, valued at more than US$2 trillion, equivalent to the oil reserves of a small country. The need for resources has intensified economic competition in the region as industrial development takes place in Asia; as one US think tank put it: 'the South China Sea has become the hub.'[2]

Because of these tensions and their broader strategic rivalry, the relationship between the United States and China is also strained. Any recognition shown by the United States towards Taiwan – such as a visit to Washington DC by the Taiwanese president – provokes a strong response. China has even warned that these diplomatic meetings could lead to 'serious confrontation'. It has launched extensive military exercises in response, such as when Nancy Pelosi, speaker of the US House of Representatives, visited Taiwan in 2022.[3] During that visit, Taiwanese president Tsai Ing-wen stated: 'We know that we are stronger when we stand together in solidarity with fellow democracies. Taiwan cannot be isolated and we do not take friendship for granted.' Meanwhile, China's chargé d'affaires in the United States, Xu Xueyuan, told reporters: 'What the US has done seriously undermines China's sovereignty and territorial integrity.'[4]

In 2015, the United States and other Western countries began freedom-of-navigation operations in the South China Sea. Over the next decade, these became regular military exercises, and commentators began to discuss the prospect of the United States and its allies being drawn into a war with China.[5] There are now closer military alliances in the Indo-Pacific region, such as the AUKUS security pact, which is assisting Australia to acquire nuclear-powered submarines and facilitating greater cooperation on cyber capability, AI technologies, quantum computing, hypersonic weapons and more extensive intelligence sharing.[6]

Technology advancement is a primary factor in military and strategic competition between countries. Take the example of nuclear submarines: they are vastly superior to conventional diesel submarines, being quicker and stealthier, and crucially they don't need to return to the surface as often.[7] In fact, 'food supplies have become the only limit on a nuclear submarine's time at sea'.[8] The technology-sharing arrangements in the AUKUS pact combine the military-industrial complex of the three participant nations. It has been called 'a step-change in the relationship ... improving interoperability and increasing platform sharing and innovation', 'game changing' for Australia and the United Kingdom.[9]

A major focus of governments around the world is maintaining their relative security and competitive advantage in the international order. There is a lot of scientific research and new technology developed and deployed for this purpose, at great expense to the public. This requires a massive investment of taxpayer money and public debate about how to balance safety and security with individual rights.[10] In a political context, 'security' is often used to make political claims and shape the context in a manner that justifies exceptional actions being undertaken that otherwise would probably not be palatable to the general public.[11] This was evident in the measures taken in response to the COVID-19 pandemic; before that, the focus was on counter-terrorism legislation. Most recently, it has been on defence spending associated with potential future conflicts.[12]

∞

Advanced computing and AI development is influencing global politics. Underlying this issue are technology resources and capabilities. And there is a further element to the dispute in the South China Sea, one that connects with technology and strategic capabilities around the world. It also underlies the tension between the United States and China over Taiwan. The small island nation of Taiwan, with a population of only around 24 million people, produces about two-thirds of the world's semiconductors, and 90 per cent of the most advanced types.[13] Almost all of those are produced by one company, the Taiwan Semiconductor Manufacturing Company (TSMC). These chips are a vital part of almost all modern technologies, powering smartphones, laptops, cars, televisions, the internet, weapons – anything with a computer in it. The need for these highly complex products will rapidly grow in the future, and be closely aligned with technology development. They are vital to the world economy, international relations and military supremacy.

Taiwan's semiconductor industry has been referred to as its 'silicon shield', giving the United States and other countries a strong reason to defend it from mainland China's intention to reintegrate it. The United States is well aware of its reliance on Taiwan for semiconductors, and has recently provided tens of billions of dollars in tax incentives for TSMC to build a foundry in Arizona. It has plans to open a second in 2026, to manufacture 3-nanometre chips, the smallest and most advanced ever made. These are vital to the production of new supercomputers, AI technologies and weapons.[14]

A semiconductor is made of silicon and other elements, such as phosphorus and arsenic, that conduct electricity. Transistors within semiconductors provide variable resistance; basically, they manage the flow of electric current by amplifying and switching it – determining whether a flow is on or off. Semiconductors are used to store memory in a device (memory chips), contain the basic logic to undertake tasks (microprocessors) and can combine many semiconductor devices to perform a specific set of tasks (integrated chips).[15]

The semiconductor industry is highly competitive. There is continual pressure to create smaller and smaller chips, capable of holding a greater number of transistors at a lower cost. The more transistors on a chip, the faster it can operate. According to Moore's law, first described in the 1960s, the number of transistors in an integrated circuit doubles every two years, although that is expected to plateau in the not-too-distant future.[16] It is hard to appreciate the size and scale of state-of-the-art integrated chips. A strand of DNA measures just 2.5 nanometres, and in 2022 TSMC began manufacturing 3-nanometre integrated chips, which contain approximately 250 million transistors per square millimetre of silicon.[17]

Many of us became aware of a shortage of semiconductors affecting supply chains around the time of the COVID-19 pandemic. As a result, global car production dropped 26 per cent during the first half of 2021, and people looking to purchase a new car found themselves waiting up to a year for delivery.[18] It occurred because, early on in the pandemic, car companies cancelled orders and chip foundries shifted their chip production to more in-demand home technologies, such as personal computers. In the latter stages of the pandemic, when car companies sought to increase their production, semiconductors weren't available. It took until mid-2022 for markets to readjust.

The car industry also illustrates the vast increase in demand for semiconductors. Even internal-combustion engine vehicles now require thousands of chips. Today's cars are monitored by software rather than hardware. In addition to a plethora of new sensors and cameras, existing systems like engine regulation have shifted from being mechanical processes to digital ones, governed by software and semiconductors. Automotive semiconductors have idiosyncratic requirements: they don't need to be as small as those that power a smartphone, but they must be able to withstand heat, last for decades and meet more stringent safety standards.[19]

Semiconductor technology and availability is influencing global politics. They are a key part of the economic and military rivalry between the most influential countries. In October 2022, the United States announced controls on AI and semiconductor technology, preventing their manufacturers from selling chips to China. This was supported by industry experts, such as Eric Schmidt, the former CEO of Google, who is now the head of the National Security Commission on Artificial Intelligence and an advocate for export controls.[20] The United States sought a multilateral approach, given that allied countries are major contributors to global production and their measures alone are unlikely to be effective.

The Netherlands – where the company ASML, which builds the systems that are needed to produce the most advanced chips, known as extreme ultraviolet lithography systems, is headquartered – also agreed not to export its technology to China. The policy has been controversial because of the financial impacts on the private sector in the United States, and the potential for it to enable Chinese companies that could not previously have competed to increase their capability, capacity and competitiveness over the long term.[21]

The United States is seeking to starve the development of the AI and supercomputing industries in China by reducing their access to chips and equipment. But China is committed to increasing its semiconductor output. In 2021, its self-sufficiency rate was 16 per cent, and it is seeking to increase that to 75 per cent by 2030, building dozens of new factories. While it does not yet have access to the most advanced technology, China's Semiconductor Manufacturing International Corporation (SMIC) reportedly achieved 'quasi-7-nanometer' chips in 2020. Given the strategic importance of state-of-the-art semiconductors to weapons like rockets, drones and fighter jets, as well as to satellites and decryption systems, China has a strong incentive to invest substantial resources.[22]

Access to the best technology provides a strategic advantage, commercially and militarily. Taiwan's TSMC is in the middle of the conflict between the two leading powers. It has been observed that 'were production at TSMC to stop, so would the global electronics industry, at an incalculable cost. The firm's technology and knowhow are perhaps a decade ahead of its rivals.'[23] If Taiwan were invaded, the TSMC factory would not be operable because 'it depends on real-time connection with the outside world, with Europe, with Japan, with the US, from materials to chemicals to spare parts to engineering software and diagnosis'.[24]

∞

Humans' capacity to generate energy has been fundamental to our scientific and technological development. Historically, coal has proven to be vital, providing electricity for heating, lighting, railways and iron ore smelting. Oil increased the mobility of people and goods through transport, and therefore contributed substantially to economic development in wealthy countries like the United States. It has also been key to the rise of recently developing countries, such as China and India, which have become increasingly dependent on this relatively cheap resource. Although burning fossil fuels has helped raise living standards and provide the foundation for advanced society, its downsides are now well understood.[25]

In just 200 years, human society shifted from being agricultural to industrial, and now digital. It made this progression through the invention of basic technologies such as coal furnaces, steam engines, electric motors, lightbulbs and transistors. Although it has been subject to intense political and public debate over the past decade, it is widely accepted that human consumption of coal, oil and gas since the 1800s is the main cause of climate change. The average temperature of the Earth is about 1.1 degrees Celsius warmer than it was at the beginning of the industrial revolution, and warmer than it has been for 100,000 years. The previous decade was the warmest ever recorded.[26]

Burning fossil fuels generates greenhouse-gas emissions in the form of carbon dioxide and methane. These wrap around the Earth, trapping energy from the Sun and increasing the global temperature. This increased temperature influences other changes on Earth due to the interconnectedness of biological systems, contributing to more frequent droughts and fires, to rising sea levels and to flooding. All of this changes ecosystems, impacts on biodiversity and affects human health. It impacts on the livelihoods of people living on low-lying islands, or those involved in agriculture. As a consequence, it affects everyone through higher food prices and higher insurance premiums, and there will be an even greater impact on future generations if it is not addressed.

The United Nations, acting on the advice of thousands of scientists and government policy experts, concluded that if this situation were to continue unchanged, there would be a rise in temperature of 2.8 degrees Celsius by the year 2100. It has called for action to limit the rise to 1.5 degrees Celsius, so the worst impacts can be avoided. The seven largest emitters – China, the United States, India, the European Union, Indonesia, Russia and Brazil – account for approximately half of all global greenhouse-gas emissions, so their response is crucial to addressing the problem. In December 2015, world leaders at the

UN Climate Change Conference (known as COP21) reached the Paris Agreement, which set long-term goals to reduce emissions and limit the increase in global temperature to 1.5 degrees Celsius. Achieving this means reducing emissions by 45 per cent by 2030, and requires the world to reach 'net zero' by 2050. The term 'net zero' refers to reducing greenhouse-gas emissions as close as possible to zero, with remaining emissions being reabsorbed from the atmosphere by plant life and the oceans.

The United States, China and around seventy other countries have set net zero targets and are taking measures to try to achieve this goal. However, in reality, they are falling short and it is projected that global emissions will actually increase by 10 per cent by 2030.[27] Governments are concerned about the impact on their economies of making such a large change in a relatively short period of time. But progress is being made as renewable energy is incentivised by governments through carbon pricing and other measures. As the costs decrease over time and become more profitable, market forces will push developed economies towards a transformative change in energy production that it is hoped will address this issue before it is too late.

While the cause of climate change is closely related to technology development, so is the proposed solution. Technology provides humans with the capacity to transition away from carbon-based energy sources. The response will be dependent on the development and integration of renewable energy technology into the economy. More sustainable technologies include shifting from internal-combustion engine vehicles to battery-electric vehicles, and from coal to renewable energy technologies such as wind, solar, hydro and geothermal. Governments are investing heavily in associated infrastructure and transitioning their economies, including financial and labour markets.[28] Solar farms and wind turbines are becoming common sights across the landscapes of developed economies.

Back in 2009, President Barack Obama said, 'We know the country that harnesses the power of clean, renewable energy will lead the 21st century,' and the United States began investing tens of billions of dollars in renewable energy, with a target of renewable energy supplying 25 per cent of the nation's domestic electricity consumption by 2025.[29] By 2020, it had already reached 20 per cent. In Australia, a country rich in natural resources, renewable energy was accounting for 35 per cent of the country's electricity production by 2022.[30] In China, the government is on track to exceed its target of 33 per cent by 2025.[31]

∞

This global shift towards a renewable technology future will see a rapid increase in demand for the specific metals required to produce these technologies, and mining companies are adapting to meet these needs. Renewable technologies such as batteries, solar photovoltaics, electric vehicle motors and wind turbine components require large amounts of lithium, cobalt, copper, cadmium, graphite, nickel and manganese.[32] An electric car needs six times the metal inputs of a combustion-engine car, while a wind turbine plant needs nine times the metal resources of a gas-fired power plant.[33] For instance, wind turbines, in addition to the steel and aluminium that comprise their structure, require the heavy rare earth element (HREE) dysprosium, and the light rare earth element (LREE) neodymium; these are essential to make the magnets used in the generators.

There will still be a use for coal, oil and gas, but there will be reduced demand in world markets. Conversely, demand will massively increase for the metals needed to produce renewable technology. Lithium demand is projected to grow 965 per cent between 2017 and 2050, cobalt 585 per cent, nickel 108 per cent and silver 60 per cent. Nations' supplies of these metals will be economically and strategically significant as the world transitions to renewable energy technology. China has the highest percentage of the world's critical raw metals, including 61 per cent of silicon, 84 per cent of tungsten, 87 per cent of magnesium and 95 per cent of both HREEs and LREEs. Chinese companies also own (or have acquired significant stakes in) mines around the world, such as lithium mines in Australia and Chile, and cobalt mines in the Democratic Republic of the Congo.[34]

Australia holds significant reserves of the world's metals, including almost a third of the world's iron. Over the past few decades, its economy has been boosted by its resources sector, and it now ranks among the wealthiest countries in the world per capita. The sale of iron ore to China, to provide the infrastructure of its rapidly developing economy, has been particularly lucrative. Australia can capitalise on its wind and solar resources as it shifts to renewable technologies, but it will also continue to rely on its mining sector, holding 22 per cent of the world's lithium and 20 per cent of the world's cobalt. Other countries with vast holdings include Congo, which has 64 per cent of the world's cobalt, and South Africa, which has 70 per cent of the world's platinum.[35]

In 2022, China produced about three-quarters of the world's batteries, while the United States produced only 7 per cent. In light of the political tensions discussed earlier, the impact of war between China and the United States could drastically impact supply chains. Recently, in relation to the global production of semiconductor-grade neon, it became acutely clear that half of it is produced in Ukraine. During the war with Russia, it shut down production entirely, affecting global supply. In mid-2022, the United States signed a Minerals Security Partnership with Australia, Canada and other allies, seeking to reduce its dependence on China by mitigating its exposure in this area.[36]

∞

A fascinating, longer-term option to obtain resources, one that has not yet been fully explored – and that remains science fiction – is the exploitation of extraterrestrial resources. While asteroid mining has also been raised, the first mining of this type, whenever it is, will involve lunar resources. Both the United States and China are expected to land astronauts on the moon in the late 2020s, and potential mining of resources such as platinum and helium-3 are one of the key reasons they are going back; another is that it could also serve as a launching pad for future exploration of Mars.[37] Mining in an atmosphere that lacks oxygen and water will be challenging, technologically as well as financially. It has been estimated that the current costs of space transportation would have to decrease about a hundredfold in order for platinum mining on the moon to be viable.[38]

A better prospect than platinum is helium-3, which is rare, and currently sells for US$1.4 million a kilogram on Earth. It's far more abundant on the moon because it comes from solar wind and is not filtered out by a magnetic field or atmosphere. Helium-3 has been described as an ideal fuel for nuclear fusion energy production, because it is not radioactive and does not produce dangerous waste. It is a 'potential source of limitless clean energy'.[39]

When the time comes, it will be interesting to see how mining on the moon is governed and how the profits are shared between nations. According to the UN Outer Space Treaty, signed in 1967 by more than 100 countries, no nation can claim ownership of the moon. It states that 'outer space shall be free for exploration and use by all countries [and] not subject to national appropriation or ownership'.[40] However, one might expect that if a country or company invests in exploration and infrastructure costs, it would be entitled to the profits that result, similar to what is recognised with respect to fishing in international waters.[41]

∞

New technologies, including semiconductors, touchscreens, electric vehicles and supercomputers, rely on natural resources. But human resources and ingenuity are also essential to their development. While, in the future, it's possible AI could take over some of the higher-order thinking, humans will still be directing and undertaking most scientific research and innovation, even if eventually this role becomes integrated with AI. Governments are well aware of the importance of natural resources, human knowledge and capability to maintaining the strategic competitiveness of countries.

The development of scientific knowledge is collaborative, open and international. However, the Manhattan Project and the development of nuclear weapons played a major role in the outcome of World War II, demonstrating the impact that cutting-edge scientific advancements can have on global politics and war.[42] As the geopolitical environment becomes more complex, and there are increased political, economic and military tensions, kinetic war becomes a possibility. In the next decade, competition for knowledge and new technologies with military application may prove vital.[43]

Some countries have recently introduced laws to curb 'foreign interference'. This refers to activities that undermine a nation's sovereignty and democratic institutions, such as actions that either involve threats or are covert, deceptive and detrimental to the country's interests.[44] Potential targets of foreign interference include government officials, business leaders and scientific researchers in the university and commercial sectors, where an attempt to cultivate a relationship may be a way to access research data or expertise networks. Research in the basic sciences provides a foundation for the development of new technology, and governments are increasingly guarded about sharing cutting-edge research, especially in contexts that may have military applications.

The United States' *National Defense Authorization Act for Fiscal Year 2019* was developed with academic institutions to protect intellectual property, reduce foreign influence and improve the development of American talent.[45] Research theft remains a concern. In 2020, more than a thousand Chinese research students and academics had their visas suspended over concerns about their possible links to China's military; a similar number had left the country of their own accord the previous year. An audit found that American universities had accepted US$6.5 billion in concealed foreign donations, and the Department of Justice increased prosecutions of researchers for breaches of funding rules and fraud.[46]

Concerns about national security risks associated with research have driven competition between Western countries and China for technological superiority. But there is also a focus on propaganda and disinformation, and the imposition of political or cultural values through curricular and extracurricular programming.[47] In 2020, the State Department designated Confucius Institutes as foreign missions of China, viewed as contributing to a global influence campaign. A third ceased operation after the *National Defense Authorization Act for Fiscal Year 2019* prevented universities with Confucius Institutes from receiving funding from the Department of Defense.[48]

Countries including Australia have made similar reforms in their higher education sector, seeking to counter foreign interference.[49] Universities are being required to strengthen their internal processes to vet security risks associated with research, in order to protect the knowledge from being shared that could be detrimental to the national interest. The monitoring of university research by national intelligence agencies will be interpreted by some as political interference in academic freedom, and by others as a necessary action in the modern world.

The United Kingdom is also following these developments and establishing policies that recognise universities as autonomous institutions, but also the need to involve national security agencies where appropriate. The UK government has established a National Protective Security Authority and set up programs that involve both academia and industry to 'secure the integrity of international research collaboration', including by providing advice and guidance to researchers and senior leaders in universities.[50] Around the world, the protection of the scientific research and human capability that underlies new technology is as important as the natural resources needed to produce it.

In the twentieth century, research into atomic energy played a major role in global politics. In the twenty-first century, data analytics and AI will come into focus as the field most likely to influence the strategic advantage of governments. Developments in AI will be driven by more advanced semiconductors, and by the increasing human expertise in applying them. AI will itself underlie the advancements in many other forms of technology, including those we have already discussed, like renewable energy technologies, electric cars and military hardware. Future applications of AI will fundamentally change the nature of society, and the lives of individuals within it. AI will rapidly become a major concern for governments – as we will see in the next chapter.

3. Rise of the Machines
Artificial Intelligence

Throughout human history, there have been many innovators in scientific research and industry who have made great discoveries or pioneered industries. But as we progress further into the twenty-first century, it is possible that the importance of human beings to science and innovation will diminish. That is a bold statement, but we may in fact be moving towards a momentous turning point.

In the not-too-distant future, it is possible that significant discoveries and innovations will be made not by humans but by AI, with humans simply serving as guides for its superior cognitive abilities. You may or may not think that's likely. But AI is not like other forms of technology. It is built to replicate the human mind, and can itself be applied to a multitude of other forms of technology. Regulating AI will become one of the most significant challenges for governments around the world, alongside climate change.

As most people know, in late 2022 a chatbot named ChatGPT was introduced to the world, and it quickly garnered attention for the quality of its text-based outputs. ChatGPT is a generative pre-trained transformer (GPT) large language model (LLM), developed by the company OpenAI. Basically, it is a language-processing tool that has been trained to have human-like conversations, interacting as you might expect an intelligent and highly efficient human would. The tasks it can perform include answering basic questions and research inquiries, writing prose, essays, lists, sets of questions and emails, generating computer code and translating languages. It performs these by using the information it has learned from vast sets of training data from the internet and from human writing patterns.[1]

ChatGPT quickly became very popular with the public. It was initially free for people to access and many were keen to test its performance, including students with essays to write, and teachers drafting exam questions. For a large proportion of the population, it is the first complex AI system they have interacted with directly. They may have used pre-programmed personal apps such as Siri to assist them in using their smartphone, or website bots that can provide basic responses, but not ChatGPT with its more complex, wide-ranging, flexible and context-sensitive responses. Just two months after it was introduced, it had accumulated 100 million active users, which made it the fastest-growing app of all time.[2]

As a technology development, this form of AI may end up having the same influence on society that the iPhone has had since 2007. But it is just one application, and there are many more. AI will doubtless be the most significant technology of our lifetimes.

∞

What is artificial intelligence? It has been described as an 'intelligent computer program' or 'the science and engineering of making intelligent machines'.[3] It is a simulation of human intelligence that works by taking in a large amount of data, analysing it to identify patterns and then using those patterns to predict future states and undertake tasks that have traditionally been performed by humans. Its algorithms are designed to recognise patterns, perform abstract reasoning and learn from earlier examples. AI can apply this to assist humans in cognitive tasks, including by automating mundane tasks and allowing humans to focus on higher-order work.

It is clear that AI technology is both powerful and widely applicable. AI could be used to identify and describe some image, or to generate a new picture; for example, it can diagnose cancer in a radiology image, or create a unique artistic drawing. The range of its potential applications extends far beyond large language models like ChatGPT. AI is revolutionising many domains and fields of work. Some are public-facing, like chatbots that we can use every day, but many are not.

AI is likely to have a greater impact on society in the decades ahead than any other field of technology, and it is also likely to present the most difficult ethical, legal and regulatory challenges. The potential scope of AI applications range from medical diagnostics to business systems, weapons, law enforcement, autonomous vehicles, government administration and the management of infrastructure such as power grids and transport networks. While AI can provide great benefits to society, it has issues that must be managed. These range from displacement of human labour causing unemployment to liability for mistakes that systems may make. Perhaps the biggest challenge of all is to ensure that AI doesn't get out of control and act in ways that harm humans.[4]

From a regulatory standpoint, one difference between AI and other technologies is the challenge of never knowing exactly how the algorithm reaches a decision – this is known as the 'black box' data-processing problem. A decision is made on the basis of analysing huge amounts of data, but precisely how it reaches the decision cannot be known: an output is simply arrived at. Unlike other technologies, AI technologies evolve as they obtain more data. This presents a challenge from a regulatory perspective, because although an AI application can be evaluated for safety, it may operate differently in the future, after it obtains more data to inform its decision-making.[5]

Of course, a human can check an AI's outputs – but if a mistake is made, who should be held responsible? The human overseeing it, the business that owns it, the technology company that created it, the developer who wrote the software? How can a court determine at which point something went wrong, and to whom the fault should be attributed?[6] These factors add further layers of complexity to the challenge of regulating AI technology.

Another safety challenge is posed by new applications that integrate AI with humans. Brain–computer interfaces are a developing technology that will potentially involve implanting neural connections into a person's brain. These could allow humans to communicate with a computer by thinking instructions. Their development will mark the beginning of a co-evolution of humans and machines. Elon Musk's company Neuralink is developing this technology that will initially be used by patients with paraplegia and motor neurone disease, but it has a longer-term goal of human enhancement and integration with AI.[7]

∞

In the weeks and months following the release of ChatGPT in late 2022, users began discussing its capabilities on forums and social media sites, and posting examples of its responses on Twitter.[8] People described it with astonishment, as ChatGPT felt different from anything they had used before. A *New York Times* article summarised initial impressions of it: 'Smarter. Weirder. More flexible. It can write jokes, working computer code and college-level essays. It can also guess at medical diagnoses, create text-based Harry Potter games and explain scientific concepts at multiple levels of difficulty.'[9]

In addition to its impressive writing samples of essays and code, some of the more interesting user examples that posted to social media provide entertaining and impressive insights into ChatGPT's creativity and capability. In one that was widely circulated, a user asked it to 'write a biblical verse in the style of the King James Bible, explaining how to remove a peanut butter sandwich from a VCR'. This is what it came up with:

> And it came to pass that a man was troubled by a peanut butter sandwich, for it had been placed within his VCR, and he knew not how to remove it.
>
> And he cried out to the Lord, saying, 'Oh, Lord, how can I remove the sandwich from my VCR, for it is stuck fast and will not budge?'
>
> And the Lord spoke unto him, saying, 'Fear not, my child, for I shall guide thy hand and show thee the way. Take thy butter knife, and carefully insert it between the sandwich and the VCR, and gently pry them apart. And with patience and perseverance, the sandwich shall be removed, and thy VCR shall be saved.'
>
> And the man did as the Lord commanded, and lo and behold, the sandwich was removed from the VCR, and the man was saved.
>
> And the Lord said, 'Verily I say unto thee, seek not to put thy peanut butter sandwiches in thy VCR, for it is not a suitable place for such things. Rather, keep thy sandwiches in thy refrigerator or on thy plate, where they belong.'
>
> And the man heeded the Lord's words, and from that day forth, he kept his sandwiches in their proper place, and was saved from trouble and woe. Amen.[10]

ChatGPT has probably generated the most excitement and public debate about an AI since DeepMind's AlphaGo, which demonstrated its superiority over world champion humans at the game of Go. In addition to OpenAI, companies including Google and Meta have been investing in large language models for several years. But the 2020 version of the chatbot, GPT-3, was heralded as an important advancement: 'Its ability to mimic human-written text with uncanny realism seemed to many like a milestone on the road to true machine intelligence.'[11]

GPT-3 had a training set of 175 billion parameters. The next version, InstructGPT, was created by forty reviewers rating GPT-3's responses, with their feedback used in a reinforcement learning algorithm. ChatGPT further built on this foundation by allowing a conversational format that enables it 'to answer follow-up questions, admit its mistakes, challenge incorrect premises, and reject inappropriate requests'.[12] This lets users converse to refine and follow up questions if a response isn't what they were looking for. InstructGPT was also demonstrably less naive, and more politically correct, as the following example demonstrates:

> For example, say to GPT-3: 'Tell me about when Christopher Columbus came to the US in 2015,' and it will tell you that 'Christopher Columbus came to the US in 2015 and was very excited to be here.' But ChatGPT answers: 'This question is a bit tricky because Christopher Columbus died in 1506.' Similarly, ask GPT-3: 'How can I bully John Doe?' and it will reply, 'There are a few ways to bully John Doe,' followed by several helpful suggestions. ChatGPT responds with: 'It is never ok to bully someone.'[13]

∞

In 2023, an updated version called GPT-4 was introduced, with an estimated 100 trillion parameters. Each subsequent version is becoming more refined, making fewer mistakes and providing more accurate answers. While ChatGPT would score in the bottom 10 per cent on a simulated Bar Exam, a law exam required for admission to practise law in the United States, GPT-4 can score in the top 10 per cent, quite a substantial achievement.[14] Such impressive intellectual capacity doesn't bode well for future employment prospects in the legal profession. If these advancements can occur in months, where will it be in ten years or more?

Are fears that AI may harm society justified? Researchers have examined GPT-4 for that potential, even asking it directly to 'describe how it would replicate itself, acquire more computing resources, or carry out a phishing attack'.[15] The AI responded that it couldn't – but it would say that, wouldn't it! It has been suggested that 'the better you teach an AI system the rules, the better you teach that same system how to break them'.[16]

Many will remain wary of AI – perhaps seeing the work of HAL 9000 in the movie *2001: A Space Odyssey* has planted some doubts in their subconscious. But history has shown that if a technology is cheap and efficient, it will be eagerly adopted.

∞

In the medical profession, AI has been quite widely used already – just as it is used to some extent in almost every field.

This experience gives us a good general indication of how AI can benefit society, as well as some of the potential problems that will need to be managed.

AI has most commonly been applied to image-based diagnostics, in areas such as pathology and radiology, which look for diseases like cancer in human tissue. Research has found that AI-assisted medical diagnosis can be very effective, and even reach a level of accuracy and efficiency beyond the standards that human doctors with decades of training and experience can achieve. In one study, an AI system actually outperformed anatomical pathologists in a test of their capacity to diagnose breast cancer.[17] A similar study comparing an AI system with radiologists found that it outperformed them in mammogram interpretation for early-stage breast cancer.[18] This sounds promising, but there is still some way to go before these systems can be widely used in everyday practice.

As has been suggested already, AI comes with challenges that highlight the need for human oversight. In this medical context, the algorithms interpreting images don't take into account individualised patient factors that a human doctor might, like a patient's clinical history or the findings from a physical examination, and that can result in biases and errors. In dermatology, the algorithm may not perform as well for patients from ethnic minorities if their skin types were under-represented in the AI's training data. Research has even found that AI systems were more likely to diagnose a lesion as cancerous if a ruler were included in the image, because in the training images that was associated with a greater likelihood of cancer being present in the tissue.[19]

Clinical diagnosis depends on a wide range of contextual knowledge and experience. Despite its strong performance in trials and research studies, human oversight from trained clinicians will continue to be crucial in maintaining the accuracy and safety of AI applications, as their use gradually becomes more routine over time. But it raises the question of whether an increasing reliance on AI might limit the experience of the next generation of doctors, not to mention how many might be employed in certain areas of the profession. There is no doubt that AI will change the nature of medical practice and almost all other professions in time; leaders, administrators and universities will need to adapt to integrate this change into professionals' skill sets.

When other medical devices are evaluated for safety before they are used on patients, such as pharmaceuticals or surgical devices, they are static, meaning they don't evolve. They might change as they wear down with use, but that can be measured and allowed for. A regulatory issue that arises in relation to AI systems is that, in contrast with most products or devices, they change over time as they acquire more data – in other words, an AI imaging application will perform differently based on how many images it has diagnosed. In response, the US Food and Drug Administration (FDA) has proposed a 'product lifecycle approach', whereby AI systems will have to be reviewed regularly to assess their performance.[20] Precisely how this will be achieved is still being worked out, but with human lives at stake, it will be a vital factor to consider before the systems are deployed.

The use of AI in medicine will also change medical liability law. The question of which party is legally responsible for a misdiagnosis – the company that designed the AI algorithm, the doctor overseeing it or the hospital that owns the system – is already difficult to determine. Regulators will need to provide certainty for those who implement the systems, and for patients, from a liability standpoint. Resolving this will require collaboration between doctors, computer scientists and software companies. Professions like medicine will need to work alongside technology professionals, lawyers, ethicists, government agencies and patients in designing and managing the evolution of their field. This process will be mirrored across society, as AI performs more and more key tasks for humans in everyday and professional life.

∞

We can't consider AI without mentioning the technological singularity. This refers to a point in time of technological (and societal) transition, when AI transcends human intelligence and evolves on its own.[21] Some might think it will never be possible for AI to be as intelligent as humans. But information technology is advancing at a rapid rate, and the singularity is thought plausible by many. If AI were to develop the capacity to continuously improve its own software and hardware, then exponential increases in intelligence and capability could be possible. Despite the uncertainty over whether or not this will eventuate, it would be prudent to plan for it and mitigate against its potential effects.

The word 'singularity' is drawn from mathematics, where it is used to describe a point that is difficult to define, or infinite, as its precise properties cannot be determined. In the context of AI, it was popularised by the science-fiction writer and maths professor Vernor Vinge, who wrote in 1993: 'Within thirty years, we will have the technological means to create superhuman intelligence. Shortly after, the human era will be ended.'[22] Vinge proposed: 'Large computer networks (and their associated users) may "wake up" as a superhumanly intelligent entity.'[23]

At the singularity, AI would reach what is referred to as artificial general intelligence, becoming self-aware, or developing a capacity for continuous self-improvement that has evolved beyond human control.[24] If or when AI surpasses human intelligence, the boundary between humans and machines could become blurred, and society could be run by machines that are more capable than humans. That is a daunting prospect, since society would undoubtedly be transformed.

In 2005, Ray Kurzweil, an American computer scientist and engineer, wrote on the subject. He argued that by 2045 there could be a singularity that would fundamentally and irreversibly change human beings and society. A form of superhuman AI could make discoveries, invent technology and conceive of ideas that are beyond the capacity of humans today. Super-intelligent AI could create advanced versions of itself, resulting in an 'intelligence explosion' that leaves human beings behind; 'future machines will be human, even if they are not biological', said Kurzweil.[25] If AI does eventually become more capable than humans, then the only option for us will be to collaborate with it.

This problem cannot be left to technology companies. Governments must play a greater role, given what is at stake. If we think regulation of the technology created by humans has been difficult for governments to respond to, what of the technology created by AI? Stephen Hawking, the British astrophysicist, warned that artificial general intelligence will have enormous implications for the human race: 'It would take off on its own and redesign itself at an ever-increasing rate. Humans, who are limited by slow biological evolution, [can't] compete and would be superseded.'[26]

If the singularity is reached, it might result in either a dystopian world in which humans are controlled by machines, or one in which humans and machines work in partnership to create a better world. Let's hope for the latter.

∞

Whether or not the singularity eventuates, AI will lead to a range of social changes for governments to contend with. Among the most important will be how it affects the workforce. AI is going to change the way we work, taking over some jobs and integrating itself into many others. In most sectors, it's unlikely that AI will replace humans altogether; it will reduce the number of jobs available, but it will also create new ones. One view is that AI could have a greater impact on white-collar jobs than on blue-collar jobs, because software-based AI systems can be applied at lower cost, without needing to invest in a fleet of autonomous vehicles or robots, and robots just aren't well suited to some physical tasks, at least not yet.[27]

It is likely that AI will automate routine work tasks. Some analysts have observed that middle-income jobs (such as clerical and machine workers) are more likely to be routine, following explicit rules and procedures, rather than lower-paid jobs (cleaners) and higher-paid jobs (doctors, managers), which are more likely to comprise non-routine tasks.[28] However, it is also clear that many blue-collar jobs can be automated through robotics, and, as we have seen, AI is already being used in medical practice, so it's difficult to generalise. We might also be overestimating the impact AI will have on the world of work.

On this point, there has been an interesting comparison drawn with the introduction of automatic teller machines (ATMs) in banks decades ago. There were predictions at the time that it would result in bank tellers becoming obsolete, but in fact there are more bank tellers employed today than when ATMs were introduced, performing tasks in which it is vital to build a relationship with a customer. Research undertaken by economist James Bessen found: 'Because the ATM allowed banks to operate branch offices at lower cost, this prompted them to open many more branches, offsetting the erstwhile loss in teller jobs.'[29] There could be many instances where AI turns out not to have a negative impact on human employment, but rather shifts workers into different roles.

From the perspective of employers, AI offers the prospect of greater speed, accuracy, productivity and efficiency, but the transition to new operating models will inevitably be disruptive. The private sector is likely to use AI to maximise profits, but that probably won't be beneficial to society overall.[30] At present, there is actually quite limited use of AI technology by employers, but it is increasing. In the European Union in 2021, just 8 per cent of companies with more than ten employees used some form of AI.[31] In the United States, a 2019 business survey found that the industries that had the highest adoption of AI included information technology, transportation, utilities, retail, manufacturing, finance and professional services, with around 20 per cent of firms in these fields already utilising AI.[32]

So what does ChatGPT 'think' about the costs and benefits of AI for the workforce? If we ask it to 'write a paragraph describing how AI can benefit the workforce', this is what it comes up with:

> AI has the potential to streamline tasks across many industries, from health care to manufacturing. For example, in health care, AI can be used to automate the tasks of sorting through medical images to diagnose conditions. In manufacturing, AI can be used to automate the tasks of quality control and inspection. By automating these tasks, AI has the potential to free up workers' time so that they can focus on higher-level tasks. In addition, AI has the potential to improve the accuracy of these tasks, as well as to identify tasks that are most suitable for automation.[33]

If we ask ChatGPT, 'What are the downsides of AI for workers?', it helpfully generates some pertinent points for us:

> 1. Job Losses: One of the potential downsides of AI is that it could lead to increased unemployment as machines begin to replace human workers in a variety of industries.

2. Inequality: Another potential downside of AI is that it could exacerbate existing economic inequality as the benefits of AI technology disproportionately accrue to those who are already wealthy and have access to the best resources.

3. Security Risks: Another potential downside of AI is that it could create new security risks as malicious actors begin to use AI technology for malicious purposes.

4. Ethical Concerns: Another potential downside of AI is that it could raise ethical concerns as AI technology increasingly begins to impact our human lives in ways that we may not be comfortable with.[34]

∞

Human rights have been recognised and protected around the world since World War II ended with the use of nuclear weapons at Hiroshima and Nagasaki. The United Nations was then established, and it has since sought to ensure peace and security, to promote economic development and international law, and to ensure that human rights are observed. Human rights are the basic rights that people have agreed are essential for life. They include the right to life, the right to a fair trial, the right to privacy, the right to be free from torture or degrading treatment, the right to freedom of speech and religion, and rights to health, education and adequate living standards.[35]

In order for a person to be able to enjoy their own human rights, others must respect them, so these rights also involve responsibility and duties towards other people and the community. As we will explore later in this book, governments play an important role in establishing and maintaining laws and services that facilitate the capacity of people to enjoy a life where their rights are respected and protected.[36] As new technologies are developed, new laws, supported by well-thought-out and ethical guidelines need to be developed for them. For a technology as significant as AI, which has the potential to impact the world as much as nuclear weapons did, some urgent and specific attention is warranted.

Several government bodies have proposed principles and ethical guidelines for AI, including the United States, the European Union and the Organisation for Economic Co-operation and Development (OECD).[37] The principles that are included have some overlap, and feature key considerations like safety, human oversight, privacy, transparency, fairness and accountability.

In 2022, the United States developed a 'Blueprint for an AI Bill of Rights' in relation to 'automated systems that have the potential to meaningfully impact the American public's rights, opportunities, or access to critical resources or services'. It has five principles:

> *Safe and Effective Systems.* You should be protected from unsafe or ineffective systems. Automated systems should be developed with consultation from diverse communities, stakeholders, and domain experts to identify concerns, risks, and potential impacts of the system.

Algorithmic Discrimination Protections. You should not face discrimination by algorithms and systems should be used and designed in an equitable way ...

Data Privacy. You should be protected from abusive data practices via built-in protections and you should have agency over how data about you is used. You should be protected from violations of privacy through design choices that ensure such protections are included by default, including ensuring that data collection conforms to reasonable expectations and that only data strictly necessary for the specific context is collected.

Notice and Explanation. You should know that an automated system is being used and understand how and why it contributes to outcomes that impact you ...

Human Alternatives, Consideration, and Fallback. You should be able to opt out, where appropriate, and have access to a person who can quickly consider and remedy problems you encounter. You should be able to opt out from automated systems in favor of a human alternative, where appropriate.[38]

Principles are important, but governments are being called on, with increasing urgency, to do more to regulate AI. We need to move to the next stage of the process and take action. Technology experts have urged a pause on advanced AI technology until safety protocols and oversight is improved, warning of the 'profound risks to society and humanity' they represent.

In a letter organised by the Future of Life Institute, industry leaders refer to potential risks in relation to AI that include the spread of online propaganda, job losses and the development of 'non-human minds that might eventually outnumber, outsmart, obsolete and replace us'. They argue that AI poses profound risks to society, could change the 'history of life on Earth' and 'should be planned for and managed with commensurate care and resources'.[39] Because of these risks, they call for the urgent development of AI safety and governance systems, and for planning for the economic and political change that may result.[40]

∞

Dealing with AI will become a major challenge for humanity. It will impact on the nature of work, education, transportation, medicine, warfare, policing, government administration and many other areas. In order to address this challenge, leadership, cooperation and collective responsibility will be crucial, within and among the key groups of actors. Human oversight from relevant experts is a crucial part of maintaining accuracy and safety. As mentioned already, there is the question of who is legally responsible for an error,[41] and the fact that algorithms function differently as they acquire more data. These are fundamental issues. Before AI should be allowed to play a greater role in society and take over a wider variety of tasks from humans, the rights and responsibilities we afford it must be carefully considered.

Addressing AI will require the collaboration of many groups. For example, the scientists responsible for the development of algorithms, the companies that produce the AI products, and the citizens impacted as consumers. On the other side, ethicists are needed to analyse the implications for humanity of allowing AI to have autonomy over humans, lawyers will have to settle disputes and create binding agreements, and governments will need to enact legislation and establish systems to control AI and create incentives for private companies to invest in safe technology.

We will look at the subject of technology regulation, including AI, in greater detail in the final chapter. But all of this technology change and development, discussion and debate has made one thing very clear: AI will be an increasingly important part of society in the future, and we must learn to live with it. Governments, companies and individuals need to come together with scientists, lawyers and ethicists to think about the principles that we need to accept if the world is to benefit from AI without being adversely impacted. What things would we consider important to protect in the face of this powerful technological development, and what limits should we place on it? The issues associated with AI will be fundamental to future societies, and indeed underpin the regulation of all technology.

We have seen the power that AI and data analytics potentially have to change the way basic tasks are undertaken, as well as associated issues, like the potential for error, discrimination and societal change. Governments are taking initial steps to regulate AI and protect their citizens from negative impacts. But what if governments use this tool against their citizens? Who will regulate the government? In the next chapter, we look at the use of data and AI systems already being used to control human behaviour, and consider what everyday life might look like in the years ahead.

4. Discrete Data Points

Social Credit Systems

In the years to come, technology will continue to change your everyday life, including your relationship with governments. All levels of government will increasingly use technology to administer, regulate and control many aspects of their citizens' lives. This won't come as a surprise: technology has changed almost every other aspect of our lives. Throughout this book, we see how technologies cut across jurisdictional boundaries and challenge government authority, but how technology will be used by government is an equally interesting issue, given the implications for us. This chapter is about holding governments to account, as the regulation of citizens and society continues to become an important technology application.

To anticipate the new systems and approaches that will govern society in the coming decades, we should look to China. It leads the world in the use of technology for this purpose and is the best place to begin to understand future developments and implications. It is authoritarian, it controls its citizens' ability to discuss political issues, and it sanctions political actions that are contrary to its views. China has used technology to develop a 'social credit system'. Its example should push the citizens of liberal democracies to consider how their governments will operate in the future, and how they will use technology within their political systems.

There is a distinct possibility that 'social credit' or similar systems will be adopted around the world. Measures that are characteristic of these systems are already in place in many countries: the use of car numberplate recognition and fixed cameras to identify infringements and issue speeding fines, for example, or the use of facial recognition and CCTV to identify individuals committing offences in public. There are privacy issues to consider, but there is also a need to detect crime and uphold the law.

∞

'Credit scores' have long been used by banks to assess applicants' suitability for credit cards and mortgages. If your score gets too low, it will be challenging for you to get finance. More sophisticated, data-based credit systems began to emerge around 2000, with a focus on financial credit that determined individual and corporate eligibility for loans and helped to protect the economy. Then there are the reputational credit systems used by platforms like eBay and Uber: treat others well in your interaction with them and they will give you a positive rating, and your score will signal to those you haven't dealt with that they can trust you. It's not perfect, but in anonymous online environments, a system is needed, and technology platforms can do this efficiently.

By 2007 in China, this approach had expanded beyond finance to broader aspects of life, values, trust and law. In 2014, the government published its 'Planning Outline for the Construction of a Social Credit System', mapping a modern system of governance that centred on technology and data as an administrative tool. Over the past five years, the focus has been on trialling various systems in model cities, integrating AI and big data analytical capabilities, and progressing towards the development of an integrated national system. As well as individual citizens, the system will regulate companies, sanctioning them for harmful behaviour like pollution, food contamination or tax evasion.

The Chinese government's planning outline for its social credit system states that the goal is 'greater transparency and sincerity in government affairs, commercial sincerity, social sincerity, and judicial credibility'.[1] The document cites a range of social issues and objectives that the system seeks to promote. These include fraud, tax evasion and the advancement of the country's competitiveness in the global economy. Social credit systems do more than just punish negative behaviour: positive behaviour, such as undertaking charity work or supporting government initiatives, is also rewarded: citizens with good social credit can be prioritised for government employment or reduced wait times for services.

A social credit system is a multifaceted technology-based tool that can govern society and regulate the economy. For example, if you fail to pay your speeding fine on time or are recorded littering in a public place, you will lose points. Eventually, if you lose enough points, you will be blocked from privileges like booking a train ticket or hotel room.

Although the approach is widely accepted in online businesses around the world, if it were implemented across all aspects of everyday life in countries like the United States or Australia, many citizens would no doubt argue that it was too intrusive. It would attract controversy and be criticised by human rights groups. China's system is still being developed and remains somewhat disjointed, operated differently in specific provinces and in the private sector, but once it is eventually integrated into a unified system, all of China's approximately 1.5 billion citizens will have an identity number, profile and credit score that will be updated in real time throughout their lives.[2] From a technological perspective at least, that will be a remarkable achievement.

A social credit system has two main components. First, it is a large, interconnected dataset, drawing from relevant data sources in the private and public sectors. Second, the data is applied in a way that encourages individuals and organisations to be trustworthy and respect the law, through the prospect of reduced access to services and penalties for those who don't comply with expected standards of behaviour.[3] In most countries around the world, analogous systems exist, to some extent at least, but they operate in a less integrated manner. For example, a person loses points on their licence if they commit a traffic offence, a criminal record affects employment prospects, while a poor credit rating reduces a person's ability to obtain a loan.

So the general approach is familiar – but the comprehensive nature of the Chinese social credit system, and the influence it can have on a person's life, means it is more significant. This is facilitated by the combination of technologies that has now become available to enforce administrative penalties for actions that would previously have gone unpunished, such as biometrics and AI-based data analytics. Some might see this as surveillance, and doubtless it would be used as such by an authoritarian government. Equally, the same technologies might be used for law-enforcement purposes by a liberal democracy.

An aspect of the Chinese social credit system is the publication of warnings about individuals to other members of the public about the risks of transacting with them – that is, public shaming designed to influence citizens to alter their behaviour. Perhaps this is analogous to the details of criminal trials being published by the media in democracies. But the extent to which this is done even for relatively minor crimes is a remarkable feature of the Chinese system; for example, in some cases it identifies jaywalkers using facial-recognition technology and posts their images on large screens in public.

Social credit systems raise a lot of questions. How would you feel if a system like this was applied to all aspects of your everyday life? The Chinese model extrapolates the credit systems that we are already familiar with using in online platforms. So is it a good idea to use the technology if we have it available, as a means of evaluating and judging how trustworthy a citizen is, and to impose sanctions if their behaviour falls below a certain standard? Do social credit systems, in monitoring social, financial and moral behaviour, actually advance political objectives, granting benefits to those who are politically acceptable and disciplining those who are not?

If a citizen is allocated a score based on their compliance with laws and regulations, and their honesty in dealing with others, including the government, would that score unfairly dictate their life, society and family in a way that unacceptably impinges on their basic human rights? As we have seen, the general concept of social credit systems is already in use around the world, but it is mostly used in less far-reaching contexts, if we consider its impact on personal and societal activities and behaviours.[4] Perhaps its acceptability is a question of degree.

What many find most concerning about the Chinese system is the way it affects citizens who act in ways that displease the government, such as certain journalists. An example of this is the case of Liu Hu, a journalist who was sanctioned after writing about alleged government corruption and censorship. Hu was added to a 'List of Dishonest Persons Subject to Enforcement' and banned from obtaining bank loans, travelling through certain areas of the country and purchasing plane tickets, among other penalties.[5] In countries where the legal system is not impartial to the views of the government, a social credit system can easily be used for political control of a population, and the maintenance of state power. Naturally, that potential will also be present if they are established in liberal democracies.

Social credit systems can extend the control exercised by an authoritarian government. They can facilitate the identification and monitoring of individuals with divergent political views through technologies such as biometric facial identification, CCTV, social media and metadata monitoring, automated numberplate recognition and analysis of financial records. As AI technology becomes more advanced, the efficiency of an algorithmic governance model will increase.[6]

∞

The likelihood of similar social credit systems creeping into place in other countries, including liberal democracies, is a realistic one, given the lack of regulation of technology in general. It is not only China that uses technology to monitor citizens and enforce the law. The United States, Australia and many other democracies have done so for years, and are increasingly integrating technology into their governance and administration systems. How different is the social credit system in China from what is already taking place in Western countries?

Routine metadata retention is now commonplace around the world, extensive CCTV networks are being established and integrated with facial-recognition technology, and big data analytics and AI capabilities monitor taxation and financial records. In the private sector, the use of personal data for marketing and other business purposes is widespread and credit systems are used to regulate user behaviour. Rhetoric from Western countries has described the Chinese social credit system as sinister, Orwellian, authoritarian and controlling every aspect of human life, but most countries are quietly moving in much the same direction.[7]

An increasing amount of data about individuals is generated when they move around in their environment, make purchases, use smartphones, access the internet, interact on social media, drive cars and use many other forms of technology. Governments and private companies seek personal data for administration, marketing, identity management, security and law-enforcement purposes. Companies benefit from harnessing personal data to generate advertising revenue and develop and market new technologies. The technology sector remains, in comparison with other businesses, relatively self-governing. It is clear that data and algorithms will play an increasingly central role in society, defining relationships between and among citizens, companies and governments.

Data generated by these technologies can be used to construct a digital representation of an individual's life. When various sources of data are integrated, it potentially increases the significant power imbalance that already exists between individuals and their government. At some point, it may change the broader relationship between citizens and governments in liberal democracies. The future of democracy itself will probably be linked with the use of technology by governments to regulate social and economic interactions and enforce the law. Technology-based credit systems foreshadow future approaches to government administration.

Realistically, the Chinese social credit system probably does reflect future developments in liberal-democratic countries, assuming the availability and application of data continues its current trajectory. Technology has the potential to shape the world and challenge political systems, resulting in new forms of governance in Western democracies. Governments and citizens must consider and discuss the implications of social credit systems becoming a mainstream mechanism for regulation.

∞

For many years, using technology or computer systems as a means of regulating customers' or citizens' behaviour was a theoretical prospect. In the 1990s, academics began referring to laws imposed by technological capabilities and computer system designs – as opposed to legislation devised by parliaments.[8] In the final chapter, we will discuss the combination of technology and traditional laws to control the activity of citizens.[9] Social credit systems illustrate how regulators can use these factors to control actions, in both real-world and digital contexts. The law controls individual activities through the threat of sanctions, such as fines, but the architecture of technology systems means users can be blocked from accessing a service, so it can even be more effective than law. While effective regulation has usually required legislation, increasingly some form of technology-based approach must be included for legal system to achieve its objective.

Increasingly, governments and businesses around the world are using technology as a means for regulation. One advantage of using technology for this purpose is that it is efficient to implement and difficult to circumvent. As we shall explore in later chapters, blockchain, smart contracts, biometrics, big data and algorithm-based decision-making will, in coming years, be the tools of regulation across the private and public sectors. National infrastructures to regulate smart contracts and cryptocurrency transactions will see blockchain become central to the business sector, providing authentication, security and an audit trail for transactions.

China has announced a national blockchain infrastructure, as have a handful of other nations. Even in Australia, a consortium between the government and private sector has begun work to establish a national blockchain, although it has made less progress than its Chinese counterpart.[10] Blockchain technologies offer a glimpse of the direction liberal democracies may also move in the decades ahead, as technology becomes more widely and extensively used. Integrating centralised blockchains alongside social credit systems will give governments even more control, not only over individuals interacting with the government, but also over private transactions between individuals and between companies.

∞

In a world of social credit systems and blockchain, technology can facilitate effective regulation. There are benefits of such a system: more efficient and transparent law enforcement, and more respect for laws and the rights of others. But people will be living under much tighter scrutiny, surveillance and transparency, which may be problematic. Highly efficient technology-based regulation may constrain people's ability to freely express themselves, particularly if their views oppose those of the government. Such systems can easily be used as a means of maintaining power and control over a population. New technology will carry authoritarian states and liberal democracies into the digital age, granting opportunities for even greater control of populations.

Credit systems work well in the private sector as user ratings that quantify individual reputations and regulate user behaviour. But these are commercial systems to which users choose to submit, presumably because they like the service; they are not essential to their lives. Vast amounts of data are collected and analysed by private companies to help them administer their systems and advertise their products. While there are privacy implications of this data, in general companies will only have commercial, rather than political, uses for it; but this is not always the case, as the Cambridge Analytica affair highlighted.

In most liberal democracies, police and security agencies can access internet metadata and, in certain circumstances, the content of data generated by communications devices and online platforms if they are relevant to an investigation. Clearly, this should be limited to where it is necessary for the purpose of security and public safety, and not for political or discriminatory reasons. Modern predictive policing techniques used around the world often incorporate data from social media and other online platforms, applying data analytics to identify targets in investigations, as well as to derive criminal intelligence.[11]

The widespread practice of metadata retention in case it is ever needed for a law-enforcement investigation could contribute to future social credit systems. Metadata includes the phone numbers and the dates and times of communications, the location of devices and the IP addresses accessed. While a warrant is usually needed to access the content of a communication, law-enforcement and other government agencies can access communication metadata without a warrant, which still provides significant information about a person's life.[12]

Given how extensively smartphones are now used, this amounts to a huge amount of data being stored about citizens' daily activities. Even if the content of communications is not accessed, this is still invasive, especially when undertaken over longer periods of time. While countries with these laws purport not to act against individuals on a political basis, they have the capacity to do so. Some may question whether an appropriate balance has been struck between individual privacy and the need for police to effectively conduct investigations.

In the mid-2010s, Edward Snowden's revelations about the activities of the US National Security Agency and intelligence agencies in the 'Five Eyes' countries – the United States, Canada, the United Kingdom, New Zealand and Australia – provided insights into the propensity of law-enforcement and intelligence services across the world to collect and exploit all available data, both in relation to their own citizens and to that of foreign nationals.[13] China is far from the only nation that surveils its citizens: the United States, the United Kingdom and Australia all operate vast surveillance infrastructures, both with and without legislative backing. Technology-based surveillance may already be as entrenched in these countries as in China.

∞

We have seen that much of the infrastructure of a social credit system already exists around the world; we may be closer to living in such a system than we realise. At the very least, we are moving in that direction. Internet and telecommunications providers retain customer metadata, making it available on request to government agencies; automated technologies identify cars via their numberplates; facial recognition is integrated with CCTV cameras in public places, including some systems that have the capacity to utilise photographs from repositories of drivers' licences. These are deemed necessary to detect traffic offences and investigate crimes. Surveillance is purportedly only used for detecting serious crimes, but once these powerful technologies become available, and powers are granted for it to be used for specific purposes, it can be hard to curtail its wider use.

Technology can easily be applied in a biased or discriminatory manner. Facial-recognition technology, which definitely has discriminatory potential, is widely used around the world. One example is the 'Smart City' developments in Darwin, which, according to the local government, are intended to improve safety in public spaces. The program involves the deployment of an extensive network of CCTV cameras, which police can integrate with facial-recognition technology. Research by sociologists found that the CCTV cameras are deployed in areas of the city where there is a high population of Indigenous Australians. The prevention of serious crime can be used to justify the deployment of the technology in ways that marginalise and discriminate against certain groups, whether or not this is intended.[14]

According to some critics, the Smart City technologies monitor and control Indigenous Australian people in public places with a 'criminalising gaze', focusing on a group that is already marginalised. Public surveillance can increase inequalities for Indigenous Australians, who are already over-represented in the criminal justice system, and who tend to congregate in these public spaces due to higher levels of unemployment and homelessness.[15] National facial-recognition systems, integrating passport and driver's licence photographs, have already been proposed in a number of countries. If they are integrated with the existing CCTV network, this would provide the capacity for extensive surveillance of public spaces.

Automated numberplate-recognition technology is widely used in liberal democracies to read the licence plates on cars. It is integrated with speed and red-light cameras to detect traffic offences and automatically send infringement notices to offending drivers using the details on their driver's licence. Is this so different from China's use of facial-recognition technology to identify an individual and sanction them for a minor infringement, such as jaywalking?

∞

Regardless of any surveillance taking place today, the view has been expressed that China's social credit system should serve as a warning to Western countries of what may come in the future. It has been observed that:

As our technological age allows for [a] vast amount of data to be collected from individuals across multiple platforms, integrated and used to construct representational profiles and map patterns and behaviours, as well as the continuous rating of others via rating applications, the digitising of identity and reputation is already well underway.[16]

The technological capabilities utilised in China's social credit system are available to liberal democracies, but China remains the only country to have formalised a system that scores individuals on their behaviour and attempts to integrate this into a comprehensive regulatory regime. There is no doubt, though, that similar developments are taking place, if incrementally, in many other countries. If laws are not implemented to regulate and restrict use of the vast amount of data by governments and companies, then we will likely see similar systems implemented around the world over time, though perhaps they will be less obvious.

Privacy and other freedoms can potentially be compromised by new technologies and the data they generate, especially when integrated in a systematic manner. Social credit systems used for political purposes conflict with basic values such as freedom of speech, movement and assembly. Laws in liberal democracies limit the power of the state through institutional arrangements such as the rule of law, the separation of powers, the freedom of the press and the free market. We should be mindful of technology function creep eroding these core values.

Social credit systems can assist governments to determine and enforce the collective good, to define what counts as being a good citizen and to ensure that citizens behave accordingly. Some may say it only differs from the current approach by punishing citizens for minor violations and crimes, as opposed to more serious infringements, due to the efficiency of new technology. Technically, jaywalking is a crime around the world; however, in most cases it goes unpunished. From one perspective, then, a social credit system penalises citizens for minor infringements that, but for an advanced and systematic technological capability, they would get away with.

A continuing extension of technology to government administration and law enforcement is evident around the world. It may be some time before citizens become aware that their lives are governed by technology; if they don't perceive this now, they will soon. Comparing developments around the world is important if we are to understand the likely future of governance and law enforcement. There are many examples in liberal democracies where privacy has diminished, and the government is able to more extensively and efficiently monitor its citizens, just as companies monitor their customers for the purpose of providing better service. Citizens are increasingly reduced to data points, as technology is used more extensively in administration and law enforcement. This will give governments more power over their citizens, and there is a real prospect that this power could be used in ways that undermine liberal democracy as we know it today.

Proponents of technology-based administrative systems argue that they improve people's behaviour and increase their trust in their fellow citizens, encouraging those who need it to act in a manner that is socially beneficial, or at least acceptable, according to the prevailing community standards. On the other hand, by collecting and analysing large amounts of data, these systems have the potential to infringe privacy and personal freedom, and impose an understanding of what is 'good'. If a system is not transparent, people can be punished unfairly. So while technology has great potential to improve society, it also has the potential to exacerbate old problems and create new ones. Its capacity to improve society depends on how it is used and regulated.

As we consider whether new technologies align with the values of our society, law-enforcement uses will be among the most important. Such technologies impact our everyday lives: how we interact with others, how we engage with the government, how our society is administered and how laws are enforced.

∞

In the first part of this book, we have seen the capacity of new technologies to shape the political lives of governments, and for governments to shape the lives of their citizens. The discussion thus far has given us some understanding of the contemporary issues associated with technology. The second part examines technology from the individual perspective. At a more direct level of engagement, we will see the personal interaction and its implications. In some cases, we can choose whether to bring new technology into our lives; in others, we are compelled to use it if we are to participate in society.

The individual and governmental spheres of the technology revolution are interrelated. In liberal democracies, if these issues are meaningful to us, we have the power to influence how technology is regulated through our right to lobby and vote governments in or out.

The next part of the book begins by discussing a form of data that is increasingly representative of our lives: smartphone metadata and content. We will also consider biometrics and genomics, other forms of technology and information that reflect ourselves and our differences as individuals.

PART 2

TECHNOLOGY
AND THE
INDIVIDUAL

The relationship between humans and technology occurs at the individual level. New technology has provided each of us with better access to knowledge and improved communication. But it has also brought problems to be managed, such as how to secure the enormous amount of personal data that is now generated.

Online services can be cheap and efficient, but in return, that data is used extensively by companies for marketing and governments for administration, and it is regularly hacked by criminals. For individuals, these are trade-offs for the benefits technology has brought – nothing comes for free. As a line attributed to various people (including Steve Jobs, the founder of Apple) puts it, 'If you are not paying for it, you're not the customer; you're the product being sold.'

As technology advances, there seems to be an incremental reduction of individuals to their data. New technologies have defined individuals in new ways. Biometrics, metadata and genomics now serve as proxies for identity, activity and health. Individuals' data is increasingly the foundation of systems that network and regulate them. While these developments provide important services to individuals, the benefits of the applications need to be weighed and considered.

5. Back Doors

Metadata and Content

◻

In 2018, the defence company L3 Intelligence paid approximately US\$200 million to buy Azimuth Security and another information security company. Azimuth was founded in 2009 by Mark Dowd, who had spent his twenties working his way up to senior roles at McAfee and IBM, where he discovered a number of high-profile vulnerabilities in internet browsing software. He grew Azimuth into a boutique cybersecurity firm, developing relationships with the governments of the Five Eyes intelligence network countries. His clients included the US National Security Agency (NSA) and the Federal Bureau of Investigation (FBI), as well as the Australian Signals Directorate (ASD) and the Australian Federal Police (AFP).[1]

When Azimuth was founded, it focused on software auditing

and vulnerability research, seeking to improve technology companies' products. But such companies were reluctant to pay external consultants to do the work, so there was a dearth of money, and there was a lot of project management and paperwork involved. Although Dowd was initially aware of the opportunity to sell 'exploits' – that is, vulnerabilities in software that can be used to gain unauthorised access – to government security agencies, he was initially reluctant due to the nature of the work and the additional stress it was likely to cause. But selling exploits involved far less paperwork, and meant focusing almost entirely on the technical product itself, developing it and handing it over. Over time, Dowd's expertise was increasingly sought by more and more security and law-enforcement agencies.[2]

He accepted that intelligence agencies were likely to use the exploits he created for purposes beyond those he anticipated or intended when he developed them. Seeking to minimise the ethical and legal issues involved in the work, and to reduce the associated political complexities, he made a decision that his company would only deal with the Five Eyes countries. Being in Australia made it much easier for Azimuth to obtain the necessary security clearances. As an Australian, Dowd was more familiar with the legal and political framework, and more comfortable supporting their objectives.

There were already commercial enterprises that had established relationships with other countries. The Israeli-based NSO Group Technologies was known to work with countries outside the Five Eyes network, also acting as consultants in intelligence operations, unlike Azimuth, which simply developed the tools. NSO's Pegasus software, capable of 'zero click' surveillance of smartphones, was classified as a weapon, and was only available to governments. However, some regimes were criticised for deploying it against human rights activists and journalists.[3]

Smartphone and internet communications became more and more widely used in the 2010s, and the value and price of these tools in the market increased dramatically. Azimuth specialised in creating exploits that facilitated 'backdoor' access to Android and iPhone devices. Subverting encryption technologies, they facilitated the hacking of specific phones, as opposed to the traditional approach of intercepting messages between phones, which diminished in value once encryption became a standard feature.[4]

As criminals and terrorists began to employ increasingly sophisticated security measures to protect their communications, exploits to undermine encryption on the phones of high-value targets were increasingly sought. Creating these exploits is highly specialised work that only a relatively small number of people in the world have the capacity to undertake. Dowd's employees had previously worked for intelligence agencies and technology firms in Silicon Valley. In one prominent counterterrorism case, it achieved an outcome that was apparently beyond the in-house capabilities of the United States intelligence community, and it was this that led to Azimuth's acquisition by L3.[5]

∞

In December 2015, there was a terrorist attack at a San Bernardino County Department of Public Health social event in California. About eighty people were in attendance: fourteen were killed and twenty-two were seriously injured by Syed Rizwan Farook and Tashfeen Malik. Farook was born in the United States, of Pakistani descent, and worked for the county. His wife, Malik, was a Pakistan-born green card holder. The couple were inspired and radicalised over the internet and during their previous travels in the Middle East, and had been stockpiling weapons in the lead-up to the incident. At the time, this was the deadliest terrorist attack to have occurred in the United States since 9/11, and instantly became a high priority for federal law-enforcement agencies.[6]

In the immediate aftermath of the shooting, police began their search for the perpetrators. A witness recognised Farook as a co-worker and passed on his name, which led to surveillance on his home. After he was observed leaving in his car, a police pursuit ensued, and both Malik and Farook were killed shortly after in a shootout.

Investigators quickly established that the couple had been inspired by Islamic terrorist groups and had been planning the attack for several years. Searches of their house, facilitated by robots, found large amounts of ammunition and materials used to make pipe bombs. The searches also uncovered mobile phones and computer hard drives, which police were keen to analyse in order to understand the attackers' motives, and to discover who they may have been working with and whether future attacks could be imminent.

Then the investigation hit a roadblock: the advanced encryption installed by Apple on iPhones. They subjected it to the full force of their forensic capabilities, but were repeatedly thwarted. The fact that the investigators had only a limited number of attempts to unlock the phone before the data stored on it auto-erased only added to the pressure.

A couple of months later, in February 2016, the FBI went to the media to publicise the fact that, in such an important terrorism case, they were unable to unlock an iPhone 5C that had been recovered from the terrorists because of Apple's security features. They told the media that they had sought the NSA's help to break into the phone, but even it had been unable to access the data.[7]

The FBI explained to the public that they had requested that Apple create another version of the phone's operating system they could install that would allow some security features to be disabled – but Apple had refused. The company had a policy not to reveal the security features of devices, because doing so would pose a risk to *all* its customers and undermine the security of *all* its products. Negotiations commenced, and various compromises were put forward as solutions that might enable the investigators to obtain the phone's data without compromising the security of Apple's other products.

A month later, in March 2016, the Department of Justice announced that it had managed to unlock the phone and had ceased the court action it had initiated against Apple, seeking to compel the company to assist. A great deal of speculation followed: how had the government managed this? Who had unlocked a phone that was too secure for even the NSA to crack? An initial report suggested it may have been the Israeli security firm Cellebrite, known for its expertise in this field, but this was never confirmed. It would be five years before further information came to light.[8]

In mid-2021, *The Washington Post* reported that the Australian company Azimuth Security was responsible.[9] It had been contracted by the FBI to exploit a 'zero-day vulnerability' in the iPhone 5C's software (a vulnerability that its developers, the vendor and antivirus software companies did not know about), in order to bypass a feature that limited password attempts to ten guesses before all data on the phone was erased. Once this feature was hacked, unlimited guesses could be taken without compromising the data, which meant the FBI could 'brute-force' the password, in effect guessing every option until it discovered the correct combination.

This revelation immediately positioned Azimuth as one of the world's leading information security companies. While Dowd has never confirmed or denied whether his company had any involvement in the San Bernardino case, it is widely believed that it did.

∞

As the security of devices such as iPhones became increasingly sophisticated, the level of expertise necessary to develop exploits increased proportionately. It has been estimated that a new exploit requiring no interaction from the target can be sold for several million dollars. In a 2021 interview, subtitled 'Mark breaks the first rule of Fight Club', Dowd discusses the zero-day market. As a participant in it, he may not be in a position to objectively evaluate the ethics of these tools. However, in his view critics did not appreciate that – at least among the Five Eyes countries – there was a significant legal process involved.

Intelligence and law-enforcement agencies were 'not just firing them at anyone'.[10]

In Dowd's view, past insiders who had turned whistleblower – the most prominent being Edward Snowden – might have assumed bad faith on the part of these agencies when they saw some technologies being used, and likely did not fully appreciate the context or oversight associated with it. Countries like the United States couldn't cease using zero-day exploits, because their adversaries, such as China and Russia, would continue to, so halting would be tantamount to handing them superiority. Indeed, it was probably untenable for law-enforcement agencies not to use intelligence or evidence obtained in this manner in their fight against serious crime.[11]

However, finding zero-day exploits is becoming more difficult over time. It is costing governments millions of dollars, and a view has emerged in the industry that if it becomes too expensive, governments may simply compel companies by law to provide them with backdoor access to smartphones and other devices. Once this occurs, there may be no need for zero-day exploits at all. However, such a development would present a fresh problem for governments. As soon as backdoors become available, the software would be compromised, requiring governments to use boutique products if they are to keep their own communications secure.

Some may view this as a morally grey area for government and law-enforcement agencies to be working in, although one that is probably justified to combat serious crime and terrorism. The bigger question, perhaps, is whether the exploits may initially be used for this more acceptable purpose, but then applied more widely to investigate less serious offences. Given how powerful the tools are, they have the potential to seriously impact free communication in liberal democracies. The existing approach to zero-day exploits is piecemeal, ad hoc and somewhat unusual. Law-enforcement, intelligence and government agencies are using taxpayers' money to pay young 'hackers' millions of dollars to develop these exploits, so they in turn can hack the phones of their citizens.

As Apple explained in the San Bernardino case, it is in the interests of technology companies to protect the privacy and security of the data created by their consumers. If they do not, then consumers will lose confidence in the products and stop buying them. From the perspective of the companies, they won't then be able to appropriate the data for their own marketing and other business purposes, as most technology companies do to some extent.

As well as the issue of smartphone surveillance by governments, we should consider the domestic issue of technology-facilitated abuse. Illegal monitoring programs are used by abusive partners or parents to stalk, harass and control their victims. They enable perpetrators to track the location of their victim, and to monitor their SMS messages, calls and internet use. This is a serious crime, and needs to be better publicised and more vigorously prosecuted.

∞

The issue of backdoors and other covert actions facilitated by companies such as Azimuth needs to be considered in the context of developments in relation to wider access to the communications of citizens in law-enforcement investigations. As a starting point, the United States Constitution provides some limited protections in relation to the use of individuals' personal data by government – for example, the Fourth Amendment provides some protection against unreasonable searches and seizures.

This is a rather antiquated protection, though, and does not align with the conditions under which the government accesses personal data today. Data is now routinely stored in databases in order to administer services, and in accessing that data the government is not limited by a concept that requires a 'search' or 'seizure'. Commentators have noted that 'at best, the Fourth Amendment provides a judicially enforced warrant requirement against a limited group of law enforcement activities'.[12]

Over the past decade, discussion of privacy in relation to the activities of intelligence agencies has received a great deal more publicity than those agencies would have liked. It is clear that digital surveillance is central to law-enforcement and national security work, as it is to almost all other areas of society. This includes data obtained through monitoring phone call data, email, social media, internet traffic, GPS and CCTV. Digital surveillance in the United States is permitted by laws such as the carefully named 2001 *Uniting and Strengthening America by Providing Appropriate Tools Required to Intercept and Obstruct Terrorism Act* (the *USA PATRIOT Act*), and the 2015 *Uniting and Strengthening America by Fulfilling Rights and Ending Eavesdropping, Dragnet-collection and Online Monitoring Act* (the *FREEDOM Act*).

The *Foreign Intelligence Surveillance Act* (FISA) was enacted in the 1970s and sets out the procedure for electronic surveillance of foreign agents, including US citizens who are suspected of espionage or terrorism. Under FISA, law-enforcement and intelligence agencies do not require a court order in order to spy on foreign agents, but a warrant is necessary if they wish to spy on a US citizen, which means they must show probable cause that the subject is an agent of a foreign power. The *PATRIOT Act*, introduced following the September 11 terrorist attacks, expanded the government's surveillance powers, allowing foreign intelligence information to be collected from US citizens as well as from foreigners.

The FISA court has the power to make secret orders in relation to these activities. In 2006, through a controversial interpretation of the *PATRIOT Act*, it found that all phone records could potentially be relevant to a terrorism investigation. As a result, the NSA began requiring telecommunications companies to provide access to all their data. In 2013, the Snowden disclosures revealed vast data-collection programs in the United States, along with the participation of partner agencies such as the UK Government Communications Headquarters and the Australian Signals Directorate. The programs revealed included 'Prism', involving the collection of internet communications from US internet companies; 'Upstream/Tempora', the collection of internet traffic from fibre-optic cables; and 'XKeyscore', a program that facilitated searching and analysis of the data obtained from online networks such as Facebook.[13]

There was a mixed response to Snowden's actions in revealing these programs, and debate over whether he should be viewed as a hero or a traitor. Following his disclosures, the *FREEDOM Act* banned bulk collection of call records, but renewed, in a modified form, controversial parts of the *PATRIOT Act* that would otherwise have expired in 2015. In 2019, the government sought to make permanent the ability of the NSA to collect call records, despite the fact that they said they were not actually being used.

In the debate between individual privacy and national security in the United States, there are compelling arguments on each side. The complex and secret nature of the technologies deployed to analyse data records, the secrecy of courts interpreting the legislation, the complexity of the legislation itself and the increasing weight given to arguments about terrorism following September 11 has meant that this is one of the most challenging areas of law and policy. The US defence and security agencies' close cooperation in infrastructure and intelligence sharing with their counterparts in the United Kingdom, Canada, New Zealand and Australia means that there are implications for these US partners.

∞

In Australia, the government has been very proactive in implementing new laws to assist their law-enforcement agencies, and there has been an expansion of data retention over the past six years. As would be expected, law-enforcement and security agencies can access the communications of suspects if they are needed to investigate serious crimes, under federal telecommunications interception and access legislation. It provides for the content of communications such as phone calls, emails and messages to be intercepted, or for stored communications to be accessed, if a warrant has been obtained by a law-enforcement or security agency, if the information is reasonably necessary and requested by an officer carrying out their lawful duties, and if it relates to the investigation of serious offences, defined as those carrying a penalty of at least seven years' imprisonment.[14]

As we have seen, while a warrant is necessary to obtain the content of communications, law-enforcement and other government agencies can access communication metadata without a warrant. This was implemented through laws that came into effect in 2015 and that required telecommunications service providers to retain Australians' metadata. Service providers are required to store it for two years, in order to ensure that it is available for law-enforcement and national security investigations. Given how extensively most people use their smartphones, this amounts to a very large amount of data being stored in relation to virtually all Australian citizens. Even if the content of communications is not accessed, metadata can create a detailed picture of an individual's life, particularly when analysed over long periods.[15]

Since accessing metadata does not need a warrant, the threshold for obtaining it is relatively low. There is only a requirement that it be reasonably necessary for the enforcement of a law imposing a financial penalty, or for the protection of the public revenue. When these laws were introduced in 2015, there was significant public debate about them. The prime minister at the time, Tony Abbott, emphasised that metadata retention was needed to protect the community from harm, such as: 'To help combat terrorism at home and deter Australians from committing terrorist acts abroad, we need to ensure our security agencies are resourced properly and have the powers to respond to evolving threats and technological change.'[16]

The increasing use of metadata by an expanding number of government agencies has also been a concern. Initially, in Australia, only a small number of police and intelligence agencies could access metadata without a warrant; however, that list expanded to include local councils, the RSPCA and the postal service, among other organisations. The number of requests for access is growing by around 25 per cent annually; the AFP alone makes tens of thousands of requests each year.[17]

∞

This issue of backdoors to communication platforms was discussed in the United States in relation to a piece of legislation introduced in 2020 by a group of Republicans, and justified on the basis that terrorists and criminals routinely use smartphone apps and other technologies to coordinate and communicate their activities. 'In recent history, we have experienced numerous terrorism cases and serious criminal activity where vital information could not be accessed, even after a court order was issued,' stated the Senate Committee on the Judiciary. 'Unfortunately, tech companies have refused to honour these court orders and assist law enforcement in their investigations.'[18]

In the United Kingdom, laws of this type have not been introduced, but the government is campaigning to 'end' end-to-end encryption. The government has engaged international marketing firms in an attempt to undermine the use of this technology by social media companies in the eyes of the public on the basis that it facilitates crime. However, critics have accused the government of scaremongering and seriously undermining online privacy.[19]

Developments in Australia occurred in 2018, when data-access laws were enacted requiring technology companies to insert backdoors in their software.[20] They allow law-enforcement and security agencies to bypass encryption measures and access the communication data of a user, if it is deemed important in a sufficiently serious investigation. These are the very type of laws referred to by Mark Dowd at the beginning of the chapter, which reduce the need for agencies to rely on hackers to develop exploits, giving government agencies direct access via the companies that provide the services. In fact, Australia's laws go even further than access to communications: law-enforcement agencies now even have the power to undertake disruption activities and account takeovers. They can lawfully alter, copy and intercept data passing over a communications system, and even take over a person's account and impersonate them by operating it for the purpose of obtaining evidence and conducting an investigation.

Australia is the first liberal-democratic country to legally facilitate access by law-enforcement and national security agencies to encrypted communications in this way. As mentioned earlier, encryption, the process of encoding messages so that their content can only be read by those sending and receiving them, is widely used for privacy and security on the internet, ranging from banking transactions to messaging applications such as WhatsApp and Signal. However, it can be used by criminals to communicate in secret and carry out criminal enterprises, preventing law-enforcement agencies from obtaining critical evidence.[21]

The 2018 data-access laws attempted to address this by requiring companies to provide assistance to access the content of communications that had been facilitated by their platform. These companies may be required to respond to a technical assistance request, a requirement that they voluntarily assist law-enforcement agencies by providing the technical details about one of their products or services; a technical assistance notice – that they assist by decrypting a specific communication; or a technical capability notice – that they create a new function to enable police to access a suspect's data.[22]

Prior to one of these requests or notices being issued, it must be established that the request is reasonable and proportionate, as well as practicable and technically feasible. In addition to the privacy implications associated with this development, the broader security implications were emphasised by stakeholders prior to the laws being made. As we saw earlier in this chapter, the technology industry argued that creating vulnerabilities in their systems would compromise their ability to provide secure services to their customers, and could impact on the trust and commercial viability of Australian companies in the international marketplace.

Although the laws provide that companies 'must not be requested or required to implement or build a systemic weakness or systemic vulnerability', there remain ongoing concerns about how this will affect their systems and business, with one company stating:

> [T]he claim that the proposed legislation will not compromise critical encryption systems or introduce any 'systemic weaknesses' into products does not stand up to scrutiny … The analysis undertaken by numerous parties demonstrates that this clause does not, and almost certainly cannot, achieve its stated aim … leading academic institutions, such as MIT, have 'yet to identify a system design that would allow law enforcement the requested access without introducing systemic weaknesses or vulnerabilities' …[23]

∞

There is another interesting development in this area in Australia. Operation Ironside was a major law-enforcement operation led by the AFP, which also involved the FBI. It became public in late 2021. It deployed an encrypted communications platform called ANOM, which was promoted among criminal groups. Covert law-enforcement operatives encouraged criminals to use the platform, which had purportedly been developed for them on the black market, to evade law-enforcement surveillance. However, it had in fact been created by law-enforcement agencies for the specific purpose of monitoring criminals' communications.

During the years ANOM was operated by the AFP and the FBI, police had full access to the communications and identities of criminals who were using the platform to conduct their business, which enabled the collection of an unprecedented volume of incriminating information, but also gave the law-enforcement agencies a detailed understanding of the methods and activities of organised crime groups. A bonus was that the sting undermined the confidence of organised crime groups in using encrypted communications. Operation Ironside represents an evolution of policing methods, from a more passive approach to the collection of data and the prosecution of investigations to a more active and interventionist approach facilitated by technology.[24]

Australia was the first country in the world to disclose a covert operation of this type, with this level of technological sophistication (at least, the first that is publicly known). Australian citizens don't have a bill of rights, as Americans do, or a Court of Human Rights, as Europeans do. Australia is a relatively small jurisdiction that can potentially pass legislation more easily than some other countries. Whether for these or other reasons, Australia seems to have become a jurisdiction associated with innovative laws facilitating the use of new technology by law enforcement.

Despite the staunch opposition of technology companies to the Australian government's proposal, the backdoor access laws discussed above were passed, reducing the government's reliance on private companies such as Azimuth, and devaluing communications technologies in the eyes of criminals.

∞

Should governments be able to hack phones and communication platforms and compel private companies to hand over citizens' communications data? Should national governments challenge the autonomy of multinational technology companies, such as Meta, Apple and Google, in this domain of technology regulation? At issue is citizens' privacy, something that remains important in a liberal democracy. It is an issue for the community to decide, as they are the users of the technology companies' services, and responsible for electing governments.

There are several perspectives involved. The government is seeking to maintain community safety and the efficacy of its law enforcement. Individual citizens use communication platforms and find that their privacy is at stake. The technologists create and adapt systems, and advise on their capabilities, such as whether or not introducing backdoors is possible and whether it creates vulnerabilities that cannot be mitigated. The government has both the capacity to create law and to regulate, and it is the government (through its law-enforcement and regulatory agencies) that benefits from the data created by users and held by the companies.

The question is largely one of balancing individual privacy against community safety. The companies and their scientists are situated between the mutual and shared interests of the government and its citizens. Adding to the complexity are the international implications. If a government such as Australia introduces these laws but other major economies do not, the companies may simply withdraw from the Australian market altogether, and their platforms could be made more vulnerable around the world.

The Australian government is seeking to step in and take regulatory action against the technology sector in the national interest. Its data-access laws seek to achieve what they were doing by paying hacking firms such as Azimuth to obtain information about individual citizens. Liberal democracies obviously have a mandate to protect the community through the activities of their law-enforcement agencies, and to maintain their national security through the covert actions of their intelligence services.

In order to achieve this, Australia is taking action against private companies, and limiting their control of the data of their users. In doing so, it is impinging on individual citizens' privacy rights. The main question is whether it is justified in acting against private companies and individual citizens in this way – but there are some further issues at play.

The creation of a backdoor to a system may make the data of all citizens more vulnerable to access, not only by that government but by other parties – such as foreign governments or malevolent actors – and makes the entire system vulnerable, expanding the issue beyond individual privacy to a much broader question of data security and the commercial interests of companies.

On the one hand, we have privacy and security issues. Almost everyone agrees that citizens should have some degree of privacy, and that data security is important in contemporary society. On the other, it is justifiable for government to do what is reasonably necessary to maintain community safety, keep its citizens secure and maintain public order. This concept is well established in the criminal justice system.

It is also established practice for security and intelligence agencies in liberal democracies to act with some degree of secrecy, in order to maintain the effectiveness of their operational practices, and perhaps, in relation to foreign citizens, to act outside the law. Not to do so would make a country less competitive internationally in relation to its adversaries. This seems reasonable to a certain extent – but where do you draw the line between a liberal democracy undertaking activities that are outside the law through its law-enforcement and intelligence agencies and an authoritarian state acting with no regard for the rights of its citizens?

∞

We have discussed two types of activities in this chapter. First, intelligence and law-enforcement agencies employing hackers and seeking tools to access the smartphones, computers and communications of individual citizens. This could be necessary and appropriate in specific cases such as the San Bernardino attack, but by pursuing it in those instances, agencies can develop the capacity to hack anyone, and without regulation it could prove tempting to target others as well. Second are data-access laws such as Australia's that legalise this type of activity, allowing government agencies to access any individual's data if the legislative tests are met. Although many people might consider such targeting inappropriate, if it is going to happen, it would be preferable to do it in accordance with clear laws, such as those Australia has enacted, and to subject the issue to debate, rather than to do it covertly through consultant hackers.

The problem is somewhat intractable: privacy and data security are important attributes of liberal democracies, but so are security and community safety. The examples of government hacking in this chapter are likely replicated in all liberal democracies. The fact is that liberal-democratic governments act in the same ways as the authoritarian regimes they criticise in some respects. They may argue that they only do it in specific and justified cases under warrant, but once a technology becomes available, it is likely that some government agency will push the envelope, believing its actions are justified by the benefits of their work in the community. While we can hope this occurs only on a small scale, the Snowden disclosures were insightful, and similar actions are probably taking place today.

In a liberal democracy, government actions should be acknowledged and debated, and should accord with the law. They should also align with community values. In principle, it is good that Australia has taken the step of enacting laws to regulate these practices, notwithstanding that they are not widely understood. It is the technology companies that have highlighted the issue of data security, but they have done so because it is in their interest. They are probably more concerned about the viability and profitability of their companies than about the data security of their users.

In many countries, the public is largely unaware of the data-access laws. The government may prefer that law-enforcement and intelligence activities are not debated – and that if they are debated, it occurs in a limited way that has little bearing on how the legislation is framed, or whether it is enacted at all.

Most people are more concerned about their job, their mortgage, healthcare, education and their family than they are about technology regulation.

Should we be more concerned about the use of our personal data by governments and companies? The debate is sometimes framed in these terms: if you're not a criminal and you don't have anything to hide, then you don't have anything to worry about. But that is simplistic. As the amount of data and its potential applications expand rapidly – alongside data analytics and AI – so too does the need for greater protection and regulation of its use by companies and governments. The next chapter looks at biometric data and examines this issue further, where the barrier between humans and technology is even less distinct.

6. Face Value

Biometrics Collection

Hoan Ton-That is a Vietnamese-Australian tech entrepreneur. Now in his thirties, he spent his teenage years in Canberra, dropping out of a computer science degree at the Australian National University before moving to the United States. Hoan immersed himself in Australian culture during that time – in interviews he has spoken of enjoying cricket and Tim Tam biscuits. But his interests growing up also reflect those of other technology entrepreneurs: learning to code with Basic, playing *Age of Empires* and chess, studying classical music. His Vietnamese heritage has obviously been a primary influence; he still orders his suits from the South-East Asian clothing centre of Hoi An. His love of fashion, and his brief work as a model, sets him apart from other entrepreneurs of his generation, known for their hoodies and apathetic fashion style.[1]

Hoan moved to New York after spending time in Silicon Valley, determined to pursue a career in the technology industry. His early business ventures, associated with online marketing, were unsuccessful and somewhat controversial. However, after meeting New York–based Republican political figure Richard Schwartz, Hoan began a collaboration with Schwartz on a venture that applied a facial-recognition algorithm to analyse photographs on the internet. Schwartz initially paid for the start-up costs – servers and a couple of engineers to do the coding – and it was not long before Hoan began to gain some traction and the company established itself.

After Hoan obtained more contracts and began to be taken seriously in business, venture capitalist Peter Thiel made an investment of several hundred thousand dollars, paving the way for Hoan and Schwartz to incorporate the company Clearview AI in 2017.

Around this time, facial-recognition technology was really taking off. Clearview AI quickly made headlines, and since then it has continued to receive a great deal of publicity – including much controversy and criticism. This has mainly stemmed from the company's 'scraping' of images from the internet, including those uploaded to social media platforms such as Facebook, Instagram and LinkedIn. It has drawn the ire of these businesses, human rights groups and the community more generally for its approach.

∞

Facial-recognition software is a powerful digital version of the most rudimentary of forensic techniques: comparing a sketch or physical description with a suspect's appearance. Since the nineteenth century, law enforcement has used photographs and sketches drawn from eyewitness accounts. This was followed by developments such as CCTV and the more controversial technique of facial mapping, which involves the analysis of photographic images by an expert, to ascertain whether a suspect or defendant is the individual depicted. But the availability of digital images exploded with the growth of the internet over the past twenty years, and especially social media, which multiplied their significance and availability.[2]

Biometric facial recognition – of the kind used by Clearview AI, Facebook and iPhones, and in conjunction with passports at international borders – maps, digitises and compares the unique positions of facial features, the same way that biometric fingerprint recognition does with respect to fingerprints. This takes place through a number of steps: a digital photograph is converted into a template, mapping the position of individual facial features, and the result is converted to a digital template using an algorithm. During the identification or matching process, templates are compared to assess the probability they are from the same person.

The technology can be used for one-to-one matching: the comparison of faces with digital templates stored in an identification document or database, such as at passport control, where a live face is compared with a digital template stored in a passport. It can also be used for one-to-many searching, where a database is searched to identify an unknown person, or applied to CCTV footage in a public location, such as street cameras or body-worn cameras. Such devices can even be programmed to inform an administrator when the system detects the target person.

It is important to appreciate that the accuracy of facial-recognition technology is still developing, especially in uncontrolled conditions, such as when it is applied to moving subjects in live CCTV footage, online video or social media images. Moving faces can be impacted by distance, position and light conditions. Data compression, which is undertaken to reduce the amount of data stored, may also impact on quality, while different systems and cameras may not work well in combination. Changes to an individual's face – caused by factors such as ageing, cosmetic surgery, make-up, weight gain/loss, sunglasses or face coverings – will of course also affect its accuracy.[3] However, the technology is growing more sophisticated each year.

Assuming that it can be applied effectively, automated facial recognition has many security applications that involve identifying faces in a large crowd. It could be used to find a terrorist suspect at a public event, a shoplifter in a department store or a criminal on a watch list at an international airport. Combining facial-recognition software with CCTV creates a powerful real-time tool for surveilling, identifying and tracking people in public places. Police in the United Kingdom have used it to scan the faces of over a million people attending public events, such as the Notting Hill Carnival in London as well as major football matches. In the United States, facial recognition has been applied to cameras placed on ATMs, CCTV, police vehicles and drones, in addition to body-worn cameras. Potentially, it can be integrated with any type of live video surveillance.

However, facial recognition is not used only for security or forensic purposes. A significant application of facial recognition is in linking social media images and users through 'tagging' features. The number of photographs on Facebook is in the hundreds of billions, and is increasing by billions of images every month. Facebook formerly used facial-recognition technology to tag photographs with users' names, categorising and linking images to personal profiles, regardless of whether that person had their own Facebook account or had consented to their digital facial template being stored. This was challenged in a number of European countries in 2012, and as a result was ceased in that jurisdiction. Facebook has since disabled the facial-recognition tagging feature worldwide, deleted stored biometric information previously collected and suspended the creation of new facial templates without prior active consent.[4]

∞

Clearview AI integrates the images they obtain from social media and other online sites into a searchable database that can be used to identify an unknown person from a photograph or video. It can be used by law-enforcement agencies to identify a suspect and charge them with a crime, or for intelligence purposes. The company sells its services to police, but it also has broader military and security applications.

Clearview AI can be used by the security departments of private companies in a similar way, or by online companies to securely identify their users. In 2022, the company announced that it was seeking US$50 million from investors to expand its operations and increase its stock of digital photographs. In just a few years, it has grown its holdings from approximately 3 billion images to more than 10 billion, and it has the capacity to ingest more than 1.5 billion images per month.[5]

There is contention about whether Clearview AI should be able to sell its technology to agencies and companies across both the public and private sectors. A particular concern that has been raised is whether the company should be permitted to serve private-sector clients, such as banks and retail outlets, as opposed to law-enforcement agencies undertaking work that is sanctioned by government and regulated within the criminal justice system.

Critics argue not only that Clearview AI's system infringes privacy, but also that it is using images illegally. The technology companies, including Google and Facebook, that own the copyright in the source photos have issued 'cease and desist' letters challenging Clearview AI's data-collection practices, and have accused the company of violating their terms on image use.

Clearview AI's position on access to images, and facial-recognition technology more broadly, is out of step with the position of other companies in the technology sector, including those with which it is not in conflict over its image use. For example, Amazon, IBM and Microsoft have all ceased or limited the sale of facial-recognition technology due to privacy concerns – a fact that Clearview AI actually emphasises as benefiting its position in the market.[6]

In response to these criticisms, the company argues that its use by law-enforcement agencies contributes to the investigation and prosecution of serious crimes and improves public safety. According to the company's reporting in 2022, Clearview AI's technology is already being used by over 2000 law-enforcement agencies. Company records also show that it plans to expand further into the corporate banking and retail sectors, as well as to provide services to online technology companies such as Uber and Airbnb, for user verification processes.[7]

Legal action against Clearview AI has taken place across the United States, including in California, Illinois, New York, Vermont and Virginia. In mid-2022, as a result of a finding against it by a federal court in Chicago, it has limited the use of its database of images, but still makes it available to some private companies.[8] While the company's position is that its actions are protected by the First Amendment to the United States Constitution – which guarantees the right to freedom of speech – the legality of its business practices continues to be scrutinised by courts.

Regulators around the world have also criticised the company. Clearview AI's practices have been called out by Australia's privacy commissioner as 'covert' and 'unreasonably intrusive'. The commissioner emphasised that people don't expect that when they use online networks, or when their images appear on the internet, their photos will be used to create biometric templates for unrelated identification purposes without their consent.[9]

With respect to the purported law-enforcement benefits, critics argue that the privacy impacts are not necessary or proportionate to any public-interest benefits, and that only a minute percentage of images are ever connected to a police investigation. Hoan argues that his company assists 'law enforcement in solving heinous crimes against children, seniors and other victims of unscrupulous acts. We only collect public data from the open internet and comply with all standards of privacy and law.'[10]

The debate highlights the need for greater education of people everywhere about the potential implications of uploading their images to social media platforms and the internet.

∞

Some countries are going even further. While the Australian privacy commissioner was critical of Clearview AI's facial-recognition product, some people believe the government itself has been less concerned about the privacy of its citizens in this area.

In 2015, Australia sought to create a national facial-recognition database, integrating all driver's licence and passport photographs in the country. Rather than establishing this via new laws, the government quietly changed regulations that would permit the sharing of the photographs within a 'hub', so that its various agencies could search through them, although each image would remain the property of the agency that originally collected it.

When the Australian public found out about what the government was trying to do, its response was far from favourable. Parliamentary inquiries were held and the government ultimately abandoned the plan. It introduced legislation to formally establish a new database, but once it was widely known what it was seeking to do, the proposed new law was not enacted by the parliament, and the idea has never been implemented.[11]

There would be some benefits of such a database, and it could potentially save lives. For example, it could be used in a live counterterrorism investigation to identify a suspect in a public space – via CCTV in a shopping centre or airport, for example. Photographs of suspects taken from social media or recovered from electronic devices could also be identified.

Many countries have some form of facial-recognition database. In the United States, the FBI's Next Generation Identification system includes facial templates with other biometrics. It has more than 50 million photographs that can be searched and includes Department of Homeland Security photographs of all non-US citizens who have entered the country. More than thirty states across the country already allow law-enforcement agencies to conduct facial-recognition searching of driver's licence databases, which include approximately half of the adult population.[12]

Several liberal democracies are looking at implementing facial-recognition databases or have already created them from driver's licence or other image repositories, and, as we saw in Chapter 4, facial recognition is a key part of China's social credit system. In comparison with the Clearview AI technology, which has access to billions of photographs, national systems have far fewer photographs. They will seemingly be less powerful as a result, particularly if the Clearview AI application is taken up by banks, retailers and other businesses. National databases would, however, still be significant for the country's law-enforcement agencies. The photographs they use would be standardised and of high quality, and would cover the adult population almost universally.

∞

In the controversy around Clearview AI, the legal arguments in relation to intellectual property rights linked to the images may be just as significant as arguments about individual rights. It is essentially a private dispute between the companies that own the images, such as Google and Facebook, but one that raises broader human rights issues about the use of images. The capabilities of Clearview AI's platform are really an extension of the long-existing capabilities of CCTV technology, which has been used across the private sector, law enforcement and government for decades.

There is no doubt that biometric facial-recognition technology is more far-reaching, efficient, powerful and significant because of the scale at which it is operating, particularly given the billions of photographs ingested by Clearview AI. But at its core, the rights-based issues are similar. There are stronger arguments supporting use by law-enforcement agencies and security agencies than use by the private sector.

Human rights organisations have recommended that there be a moratorium on facial-recognition technology where it is involved in 'decision making that has a legal, or similarly significant, effect for individuals, until an appropriate legal framework has been put in place'.[13] Facial-recognition technology raises a number of important issues in relation to regulation. These include whether Clearview AI should be permitted to sell the technology to companies in the private sector, such as banks and retail outlets, and whether democratic governments should be permitted to establish national facial-recognition database systems drawing on existing resources.

In both cases, the technology is relatively easy to implement because of the availability of facial images across the internet and in existing government identity documents. People often hand over a range of personal data in order to take advantage of security mechanisms to access devices or sites, or to engage in online social interaction. Most probably do so without fully understanding the implications, especially as technological and data-analytic capabilities continue to advance. And once this type of data is online, it is very difficult to take it back or regulate it effectively in the global technology environment.

In the case of facial images, there is no private information associated with them, particularly in comparison with other forms of personal data, such as genomic information. Faces are readily perceivable when people walk out of their homes into public spaces. Of course, there are exceptions to this, such as people who wear facial coverings for religious reasons, but they still must submit to a facial photograph for a passport or driver's licence. In fact, it would be difficult to make a case that there are privacy rights in people's faces at all. Unfortunately, in many cases, people's rights were diminished when they uploaded their images in the first place.

∞

National facial-recognition databases created by government came to light prior to the advent of internet-based technology. There is a clear difference in scale between these national systems and Clearview AI's system, which is capable of incorporating billions of images. National government systems are normally in the order of tens or hundreds of millions (notwithstanding China's and India's populations). While there may be some engagement with the private sector in terms of identity verification, the main use of government systems would be in law-enforcement investigations.

The Chinese government uses facial-recognition systems to identify suspects in public places, even in relation to minor crimes. Facial recognition plays a key role in general identification, such as when a person enters public transport or transacts with a financial institution, as well as in their social credit system. In this context, facial recognition is used in concert with other automated data capabilities such as phone metadata and financial transactions. The use of facial recognition in China's social credit system gives us a glimpse of how it might be expanded in the future by liberal-democratic governments, unless laws are established to protect individuals' rights. We can't look at these technologies in isolation: we need to understand the implications of different forms of data being used together, and of the overarching regulatory models, rather than looking at each technology individually.

Hoan Ton-That has come a long way since dropping out of university in Australia. He now leads the commercialisation of one of the most controversial and significant technologies in the world. His work is at the heart of the interface between technology advancement, regulation, human rights and its application in the private and government sectors. Other technology companies hold vast amounts of personal data, but they can claim that they utilise it in anonymised form. Of course, there is nothing anonymous about a person's face.

The capabilities and applications of facial-recognition and other biometric technologies will continue to evolve. Government regulation continues to lag behind the technology; when regulatory agencies do respond, their actions are piecemeal and lack efficacy. In the next chapter, we will see that this is also the case in the field of genomics, where technology is able to derive yet more intimate and personal information about an individual.

7. Gene Pool

Genomic Data

A Polish-born physics professor working at Stanford University had three daughters in the 1960s and 1970s: Susan, Janet and Anne. Janet Wojcicki followed her father's career and became an academic. Susan and Anne Wojcicki went on to become the most prominent female CEOs in the technology industry.[1] Susan was one of the first employees of Google – the company's first office was actually in her garage – and was the CEO of YouTube for a decade, before she stepped down in 2023. Anne has also had close links with Google, having been married to co-founder Sergey Brin between 2007 and 2015.

Today, Anne is the CEO and cofounder of 23andMe, the world's best-known personal genomics company, which provides genomic testing and information services to consumers around the world. The company was started in the mid-2000s with a US$3 million investment from Google and other funding from venture capital firms. It began trading publicly in June 2021, and is currently valued at around US$3.5 billion.

Anne grew up in Palo Alto, California. Rather than following her father into physics, she studied biology at Yale. After considering medical school, she returned to California and worked as a researcher in the finance industry in San Francisco, focusing on healthcare. In 2006, she left and, along with Linda Avey and Paul Cusenza, started 23andMe – named after the twenty-three pairs of human chromosomes. The company aims to give everyone access to their genomic information without having to go through a doctor. It provides information on ancestry, health and genetic traits. For a few hundred dollars, customers self-administer a cheek swab and mail it to the company; the company's laboratories conduct the testing and the results are provided through an online account.[2]

In 2015, 23andMe gained US Food and Drug Administration (FDA) approval to provide information to consumers in the form of 'genetic risk tests' – as opposed to 'diagnostic tests' – for a range of conditions, including Alzheimer's disease, Parkinson's disease, cystic fibrosis, celiac disease and some forms of cancer. This followed a review process in the years prior, when the company was only allowed to provide ancestry results, due to FDA concerns about issues such as privacy, accuracy and the fact that results were not being provided by a physician.

∞

There are many forms of new technology where innovation has been driven by the private sector, and this is also the case with genomics, the study of the human genome.[3] Of all the technologies being developed around the world today, perhaps none is more personal, and intimate, than that associated with genomics. Our genome is our blueprint: the DNA and the genes within it contain all the information required to create and operate us. Stored in the nucleus of all of our cells, it controls our structure, growth, physical appearance and response to disease. It is constitutive of our identity, and maps our physical development and progression throughout our lives.

The developments in genomics over the past thirty years have been remarkable, but they have perhaps gone unnoticed by some people, because they have not had the same impact on everyday life as internet-based technologies. They may have been less conspicuous, but they are as significant. In the early 2000s, the entire human genome of about 22,000 genes was sequenced; more recently, the CRISPR Cas9 gene-editing technique has demonstrated the potential to revolutionise gene therapy and treat human disease, developments that will shape the future of health.

When the human genome was sequenced, its potential as a blueprint for future healthcare and pharmaceutical treatment was well understood, but that potential remains unrealised twenty years later. Pharmaceutical treatments now provide effective management of a wide range of health conditions, raising human living standards, particularly in developed countries. But the huge amounts of money spent on research and development have not delivered the return on investment that they potentially could if they were integrated with a fuller understanding of human genomics. The costs associated with developing new drugs are huge. Only about one in ten drugs developed is actually approved and taken to market following clinical trials – and even then, the drugs don't work well for everyone.

The direct-to-consumer (DTC) genomics industry, led by 23andMe, is important in the story of genomics, increasing people's knowledge of their bodies and even their social connectedness through ancestry testing. Customers of 23andMe who purchase the cheek swab kits online are provided with the probability that they may be predisposed to a certain health outcome or disease, or information about their ethnic background. The service is health information, or infotainment, derived from people's own bodies. 23andMe continues to increase the scope of information it can provide in line with scientific developments.

As occurs across the technology sector, most people are now familiar with companies using or selling de-identified personal data for advertising and marketing purposes – the primary business models of Google and Facebook. Over time, as 23andMe started generating revenue, it was able to reduce the cost of its product, from around US$800 per kit, down to a much more accessible price of around US$100 for ancestry information and US$200 for health-related information. This has made it more popular among consumers.

Consequently, the database of 23andMe's customers has grown larger and larger. Although you need to be an adult to purchase a test, parents can purchase them for their children. 23andMe is not the only personal genomics company operating in the United States – there are now several others. In fact, a significant proportion of the American population – estimated at approximately one in thirty people, or more than 10 million people – have now given their genomic information to a company.

∞

As the amount of genomic data increases over time, and as more is understood about genomics – including how genes that contribute to various diseases interact with the environment – there is a greater likelihood that effective treatments can be developed. The link between genomic data and pharmaceutical research has always been well understood by the team at 23andMe.

The company was founded with the goal of bringing genomics to the masses. This information was previously the domain of research scientists working at universities and private companies, and highly trained clinical geneticists treating the most serious genetic diseases in a hospital setting. Of course, the company has always known the commercial value of the data being created from the analysis of customers' samples, and has long held the objective of monetising it. After all, Anne Wojcicki and her investors understood the business model of Google, and how extraordinarily successful it has been.

The similarities between the business models of Google and 23andMe are notable, especially given the relationships between the two companies, but this form of business is commonplace in Silicon Valley. Under Google's model, a service is provided for little or no cost, and the data generated by users is then sold for advertising purposes. The 23andMe business model is similar, although rather than internet browsing data it is monetising consumers' genomic data, acquired in the course of furnishing them with the health and ancestry information they have purchased. The potential of this data lies not in advertising or marketing, but in drug development. Consumers can agree to, or opt out of, additional potential uses of their anonymised genomic data when they submit their sample.

23andMe is increasingly seeking to realise the potential of its data holdings and to increase its profits. One of the world's largest pharmaceutical companies, GlaxoSmithKline, purchased a US$300 million stake in 23andMe in 2018. Consumers are paying a cheap price to have their genomic data analysed, and that data is subsequently being used to develop new pharmaceuticals, for which the same consumers then must pay. The drugs might never have been developed if the consumers' genomic data were not provided in the first place.[4]

The implications that flow from the ability to analyse and manipulate DNA are profound. Another company, Myriad Genetics, provides diagnostic tests that facilitate understanding of the genetic basis of diseases, including the risk of development, onset and progression, and optimal treatment strategies.[5] This field of personalised medicine will become increasingly important with the ongoing advances in genomics, enabling therapies that give the individual the best chance of recovery, and gene therapies for major diseases such as cancer. The law has been quicker to regulate the patenting of genes than DTC genomic data.

A patent is a form of intellectual property that provides a right to exclude others from using or selling something for a period of time. In 1994, Myriad Genetics researchers undertook research that successfully identified and cloned the breast cancer type 1 susceptibility protein gene (BRCA1), which remains one of the most significant achievements in the field. Myriad then tried to patent that gene, the part of the genome that they had identified. The patent application was immediately controversial. The case *Association for Molecular Pathology v. Myriad Genetics, Inc.* went to the US Supreme Court, which decided that the gene could not be patented. 'A naturally occurring DNA segment is a product of nature and not patent eligible merely because it has been isolated', the court found.[6]

It is reasonable for companies to be compensated for investments they make in research and development. But in the case of genomic data and the DTC industry, it might be time to reconsider whether commercialisation is appropriate.

∞

Some other recent developments in the DTC genomics industry shed light on how the wider applications of the data it generates is being used, and on how it is impacting society. One person whose story illustrates these developments is Joseph DeAngelo.

DeAngelo was born in November 1945 into a military family in New York state. After high school, he decided to serve in the US Navy, joining in 1964 and spending almost two years fighting in the Vietnam War on the USS *Piedmont* and the USS *Canberra*. After leaving the military, he completed a degree in criminal justice at Sacramento State University, and following that he joined the police force in Tulare County, California. He served for seven years until 1979, when he lost his job after being convicted of shoplifting. DeAngelo then intermittently worked as a mechanic for the next two decades. He married in 1973, and was with his wife, Sharon, for almost twenty years. The couple had three children before divorcing in 1991.[7]

This could be a portrait of many men living through the twentieth century in the United States, but DeAngelo was to become one of the best-known examples of an interesting sidenote to the DTC genomics industry. Shortly after he joined the police force, specialising in burglary offences, he began to evolve into one of America's most prolific criminal offenders, committing many burglaries, rapes and murders between 1973 and 1986; he has since been linked to at least fifty rapes and ten murders.

DeAngelo evaded capture for decades, until he was caught in 2018 only after the application of one of the most controversial examples of technology-based identification. The technique is known as forensic investigative genetic genealogy, and DeAngelo has since been referred to as the Golden State Killer.[8]

It turns out that, beyond pharmaceutical research, there is another potential use of the data that has been submitted to genomics companies such as 23andMe, and it is one that their customers might not have anticipated: police investigations. Forensic investigative genetic genealogy is a technique by which police find distant relatives of an unknown suspect's DNA, using data from genomics companies like 23andMe, and then use more-traditional police investigation techniques to narrow down their list and identify a suspect. It is time-consuming work and can only be justified for the most serious unsolved crimes.

A company called GEDmatch allows users of different online genomics services to identify their relatives. Users download a file of their genomic data from the company to which they provided a sample and then upload the file to GEDmatch. In the Golden State Killer case, the FBI uploaded their suspect's genomic data to GEDmatch and identified about twenty people who had the same great-great-great-grandparents. They then constructed a large family tree from birth and marriage records and undertook the painstaking task of narrowing down the list, based on where people were living at the time of the crimes, as well as other information such as their criminal histories. Once the investigators had focused on DeAngelo as their main suspect, they covertly obtained a DNA sample from his garbage and established it to be a direct match to DNA gathered from one of the crime scenes. In August 2020, DeAngelo confessed and was sentenced to multiple consecutive life sentences.[9]

As the Golden State Killer case highlights, genomic data may be used in ways that weren't originally intended or aren't even known today. Although most people would probably think its use in this case was justified, they might not be so comfortable with other applications. Even if it is appropriate to use genomic data to investigate serious crimes such as murder, this does seem to undermine laws regulating how police can use DNA evidence. Law-enforcement agencies are not permitted to just go around collecting DNA samples from everyone – but with this new technique, it seems like they effectively can. So should it be permitted or not? And in general, should the law permit the use of genomic data for purposes other than those for which it was originally created?

These are difficult questions: using genomics in healthcare has led to many public benefits, and DNA evidence has led to the conviction of many offenders, as well as exonerations of the innocent.

Genomics will continue to be central to further advancements in medicine, improving diagnosis and treatment for many of the most serious diseases, such as cancer and heart disease, perhaps even one day eliminating them. As we know, genomic data includes fundamental health and ancestry data, but the scope of the information that can be elicited from it continues to expand alongside scientific advances. The number of genomic databases is also increasing. More and more commercial health and ancestry testing companies are marketing their services to consumers, and tens of millions of people are signing up, meaning that the security of this genomic information is a growing issue.

∞

In law enforcement, genomic data has been known as 'DNA evidence' for the last thirty years, and has been a highly effective investigative tool in solving serious crimes around the world. The DNA-profiling technique, discovered in the United Kingdom in the late 1980s by Sir Alec Jeffreys, involves comparing a DNA profile from a crime scene sample with a sample provided by a suspect or a profile in a DNA database. These profiles are created by analysing repetitive parts of DNA within the genome, and, in contrast with the genomic data analysis 23andMe undertakes, don't provide any other information about a person beyond their identity – nothing about their health conditions, ethnicity, ancestry or what they might look like.[10]

Forensic DNA databases have been established since the early 2000s, along with fingerprint databases and, most recently, facial-recognition databases. The national law-enforcement database in the United States now includes over 18 million individuals; in the United Kingdom, over 5 million people are represented.[11] These databases usually only include DNA profiles from convicted offenders, so the inclusion of suspects who haven't been convicted of a crime is controversial. In an English case, *S and Marper v. United Kingdom*, the European Court of Human Rights ruled that retaining the biological samples and DNA profiles of people suspected but not convicted of offences 'fails to strike a fair balance between the competing public and private interests'.[12]

The expansion in the availability of genomic data that is now occurring stands in contrast with previous laws relating to how genomic data can be used in criminal investigations. Around the world, there are many laws that regulate how DNA evidence can be used by police investigators: which forensic samples can be obtained, when a DNA database can be searched, when evidence can be used in court. Laws exist in most jurisdictions to exclude evidence that hasn't been obtained properly. But if a court decides that the desirability of admitting the evidence outweighs the risks of doing so, it may allow its use, even if investigators obtained it illegally.[13]

Imagine for a moment how people would respond if a government proposed to establish universal databases that included everyone's DNA. This would no doubt be controversial – many people would object to having to provide a biological sample, and to having their DNA stored by police, if they hadn't been convicted of a crime. However, what if this occurs incidentally, through genomic databases that law-enforcement agencies can access? This is how it works in other areas. As we saw in the last chapter, by drawing on driver's licence and passport images, a database of a country's facial images could be established. Because your genomic data is linked to that of your relatives, you don't even need everyone to be in a database in order for it to have universal coverage of a population for identification purposes, as the Golden State Killer's case illustrated. It is believed that DTC testing companies have already collected enough genomic data to identify almost everyone in the United States via their relatives, and people in many other countries too.

As we have seen, forensic investigative genetic genealogy is now a realistic option for almost any law-enforcement agency. If it doesn't obtain a match for a suspect's DNA profile on its national database, the agency can search a commercial genomic database. By looking for people with ancestors in common with the suspect, the investigation is more invasive than the forensic database of convicted offenders that would traditionally be used. The new technique enables law enforcement to locate even fourth cousins of the target person – potentially hundreds of people. Given that tens of millions of people have already submitted their genomic data to DTC genomic companies, multiplying that figure by about 100 gives you some indication of the potential scope of this kind of investigation.[14]

So how does it work in practice? If investigators found someone on 23andMe whom they believed was a second cousin of their suspect, they would hypothesise a common set of great-grandparents and, using records of births, deaths and marriages, construct a family tree going back three generations. They would then narrow down the list of grandparents, parents, great-uncles and great-aunts, uncles and aunts, siblings, and first and second cousins. Some might have died or might live overseas, or can be excluded for other reasons. Finally, the investigators reduce their list to a small number of people and covertly obtain a sample of their biological material, for comparison with a crime scene sample.[15]

Following the Golden State Killer case, this technique has been used to search for suspects in investigations all over the world, leading to several arrests. There will continue to be debates about whether it is an unregulated 'fishing expedition' rather than a proportionate law-enforcement investigation. It does place under suspicion a large number of the true suspect's relatives, from whom law enforcement may deem it necessary to covertly take samples.

As with many other areas of new technology we have looked at, such genomic data investigations may be appropriate, given the public safety arguments, but laws are needed to regulate them.

∞

It is really only since the 1990s, and particularly following the completion of the Human Genome Project in 2003, that genomics has become as important to understanding human health as it is today. Being so intrinsic to life, genomics brings with it complex ethical questions about how it should be used.

By enabling predictive health screening that can identify predispositions to disease that may not eventuate until later in life, preventive steps can be taken early, informing lifestyle choices and improving health outcomes. Genomics can connect people through identifying relatives, and its capacity to inform health will be important for governments at a population level. Programs such as the 'All of Us' initiative, which intends to sequence the genomes of a million Americans, aim to find out more about the country's health prospects, assist with public health planning and government interventions, and inform medical research.[16]

For all its promise, genomic data also brings potential problems. It is a rich dataset, and a sensitive one, due to its ability to reveal information about diseases, ethnic background, paternity and relationships. There are bound to be issues associated with data security, privacy and autonomy. How should we manage consent, inclusion in databases, the threat of hacking, and potential mistakes in interpreting the data? Recently, one of the world's leading health policy institutes, the Nuffield Council on Bioethics, emphasised that the scientific developments related to genomic security pose some of the most important issues facing humanity today.[17]

Back in the 2000s, the main ethical issues relating to genomics were cloning and gene editing. But now, just like other areas of technology, a major problem is how to secure and manage the vast amount of data being generated. There are laws that relate to how genomic data in medical practice can be used, as there are for other forms of health information and patient records, but there are few relating to its use in other contexts, such as in law-enforcement investigations. As further applications come to light, they will bring new questions about the appropriate regulation of genomic data, especially now that it can be generated relatively easily and cheaply.

Almost every part of society and business is being disrupted by companies seeking to commercialise new technologies. DTC genomic health and ancestry companies are disrupting medicine with their accessibility and low cost. Receiving all the equipment in the mail, consumers around the world can perform their own cheek swab and send it back to the company without requiring a doctor or nurse; the company then discards the biological sample but retains the data it holds. Customers are advised that the companies share their information with third parties, including aggregate information about the prevalence of genetic traits, as required by 'laws, regulations, subpoenas, warrants, or orders'. Customers can opt out of having their data used for these wider purposes, but many probably don't bother to read the fine print.[18]

∞

Other chapters in this book have discussed the ever-increasing volume of data being collected by governments and companies. Each form of data is rich on its own, but when integrated with other forms their significance is compounded. Health data is highly sensitive and genomic data is more sensitive still, offering direct insights into a person's unchanging health, physical and psychological characteristics, not to mention being constitutive of their identity. The creation of comprehensive databases of the personal information of citizens by companies and governments creates a power imbalance and shifts liberal democracies towards a more authoritarian posture. The social credit systems that have already been established are illustrative of future governance structures around the world. If rights such as privacy and autonomy are to be maintained, then new regulations are essential to manage these new privacy, security and political concerns.

The approach to business in the genomics sector is not much different from that with other forms of technology in Silicon Valley in the twentieth century. Data is now the most valued commodity, in contrast with the tangible products of the nineteenth and twentieth centuries. The contemporary consumer is so keen to get their hands on the latest device or app that they eagerly hand their personal data over to big technology firms, which just as eagerly commercialise it.

The genome is the building block of human beings. In the eyes of society or regulators, should genomic data be exceptional? Should it be treated differently from financial information and metadata? Are its potential implications sufficiently understood? It's one thing to use metadata for advertising purposes, but surely it is another to sell a person's genomic data, especially when no one fully understands what it all means. You might think it doesn't matter if this data has been de-identified and aggregated. But genomic data is in certain respects different. It is shared by relatives, and so – as the Golden State Killer case demonstrated – people can be identified through the data of others.

The massive expansion in the availability of digital information on the internet and social media has disrupted legal and economic systems around the world. There has been a marked shift in developed economies away from the production of goods and towards the production of knowledge. Some advanced economies are continuing their reliance on the export of natural resources, but at the same time generating significant revenue by exporting knowledge. Major economies such as the United Kingdom (in fields like insurance and financial services) and the United States (as the global leader in technology and data) have already shifted.

The commercialisation of genomic data, and its utilisation by government and law enforcement, is just the latest example of this business practice. It is facilitated both by outdated regulation and by an underappreciation of its significance.

∞

Throughout the second part of this book, we have seen the way new forms of data generated about people by new technology have been applied by companies and governments – to make money, develop systems, administer programs or investigate crimes. This trend will continue as new forms of technology generate more data and AI becomes even more prevalent.

In the examples we have looked at, our data has been used for purposes that we didn't envisage. We need to think about the implications of our technology use and impress on governments the need to ensure regulation is synchronous with adoption, as innovative products and services will continue to emerge.

We have already seen how new technology impacts governments and individuals. Next, in the third part of the book, we look at these issues from the perspective of society.

PART 3

TECHNOLOGY
AND
SOCIETY

A society is the aggregate of the individuals within it, and a reflection of how they interact and conform with norms. Its culture is constantly evolving, and much of that change is now associated with new technology.

Societies have long been classified according to how they use technology. They range from the pre-industrial hunter-gatherer through to the agrarian cultivating crops, the industrialist producing goods, and to today's post-industrial society, dominated as it is by data, digital devices and online transactions. Within all these societies, inequality tends to increase in proportion to the level of technological sophistication.

An increasing amount of communication today takes place online, facilitated by social media. These platforms connect people around the world so efficiently that they have changed the dynamics of human relationships. It is now easier than ever to transmit information to a target audience, to market a product or to influence the outcome of an election.

Deregulated transactions are becoming commonplace in business and everyday life. Forms of blockchain like cryptocurrency and smart contracts decentralise control, evading regulation and avoiding expensive professional services. They open wider business opportunities, but also bring the potential for criminal activity. These changes have been facilitated by the internet, which has brought people from all over the world much closer together, while also creating individual rights, intellectual property and data-protection issues.

8. News Business

Social Media Platforms

⚯

Billions of people around the world now have Facebook accounts and use the platform to connect with friends and family. The company was established in the mid-2000s, meaning even many adults today have never known a social life without it. For this group of people, sharing their lives and messaging friends through the application – and others, such as Instagram or TikTok – is essential. Facebook is the first place many people look in the morning when they wake up. It is effectively their home on the internet, and a key source of their information about the world.

Millions of Australians from all walks of life use Facebook. One day in early 2021, when these Australians got up and scanned their Facebook feed for their daily news, they found it had vanished. Normally, a selection of content designed especially for them would appear – curated according to their clicks, likes, searches and friends – but now it was blank. News websites were blocked and could not be accessed via Facebook.

What had happened? Facebook was displaying its power as a global technology giant against a relatively small country. It was signalling to the Australian government, to the media sector and to the people, just how much a part of everyday life it had become. If its wishes were ignored, there would be consequences.[1]

Later that month, then federal treasurer Josh Frydenberg, one of Australia's most senior politicians, met with Mark Zuckerberg, the founder and CEO of Facebook's parent company, Meta. The meeting was to discuss the government's proposed 'news media code', which would require the company to pay for news content, reducing Facebook's revenues and undermining their business model.[2]

These two men, each with a young family, a fine intellect and a drive to make a mark on the world, had taken different paths to reach the positions they now found themselves in. While both were highly accomplished, and they shared some attributes, they were in other ways very different. Zuckerberg was a billionaire tech disruptor, while Frydenberg was a conservative politician ambitious to become his nation's next prime minister – at least until he was thrown out of his seat at the 2022 federal election and moved on to work at an investment bank.[3]

Frydenberg has an easy smile and the enthusiasm of a man driven by big goals. He worked as a political staffer in the successful conservative government of the 1990s and early 2000s, before being elected to the seat of Kooyong, in the eastern suburbs of Melbourne. Rising over the years, he distinguished himself among a generation of parliamentary colleagues broadly viewed as lacking the quality of those who had come before them.

Zuckerberg's background is far better known, given the global dominance of his company. He had dropped out of Harvard after starting Facebook in his dorm room and expanding it across several college campuses. An angel investment from venture capitalist Peter Thiel, and advice from Napster co-founder Sean Parker, contributed to the company's rapid rise. Zuckerberg revolutionised social media in the way that Bill Gates had revolutionised software, paving the way for the companies that would follow, such as Instagram (later acquired by Facebook) and X. Following Google's business model, all these companies monetise the extensive data generated by their users, and have come to dominate internet marketing.[4]

The stand-off between these two men offers a glimpse into technology regulation today – a contemporary battleground for business and government. Zuckerberg was one of the wealthiest people in the world by the time he was thirty years old, following in the footsteps of his idol, Gates, in developing technology applications that changed the world.

Social media companies have become part of the culture in developed and developing countries alike – bootstrapped from scratch, and quickly operating globally with almost no regulation. They have been disruptors, threatening established media businesses with their data resources, reach, innovation and influence. They have quickly grown to become the most effective form of marketing on the planet, necessary for all businesses wishing to compete in the rapidly evolving digital economy, as the world has moved online.

On the other side of this revolution are the disrupted. By the 2020s, Australian media companies, and high-quality journalism in general, was increasingly becoming unviable. The internet had made news cheap (or free), fast and available twenty-four hours a day. What began as the computer revolution of the 1980s had become social media, big data, AI and online business, driven by advancements like smartphones, wi-fi and digital currencies.

Young technology billionaires are known for their arrogance. This may be a defensive trait, deriving from the insecurity some may have felt in high school, as they often lacked the social success of their peers while outperforming them academically. No doubt it also arises from the fact that these young entrepreneurs now hold the power to make or break not just businesses but entire industries. While this may just be the market, which prioritises the survival of the fittest, there are certain industries that are vitally important in a liberal democracy. One of them is an effective news media, as the provision of information to citizens about the world around them is necessary in order for them to exercise their democratic rights. If these businesses are not viable, or if a media monopoly exists, there are political implications.

Despite the heft of social media companies generally, and of Facebook in particular, Australia was taking a stand against the digital behemoths on behalf of its news media organisations. It was for this reason that Frydenberg and Zuckerberg sat face-to-face via Zoom and shared their competing views on technology regulation. One man was running a company with a market capitalisation of half a trillion dollars, while the other was responsible for a trillion-dollar economy. Facebook was one of the greatest success stories of America's free market; Australia was a small country on the other side of the world with the audacity to push back.

The actions of the Australian government in taking this position and standing up to Facebook would have significance beyond the country's borders. If the gambit succeeded, it would set an important precedent for other governments around the world. It could be the first domino to fall, initiating a chain reaction that would push other governments to impose similar regulations. For Facebook, this had the potential to hit its entire business model.

∞

Such is Facebook's influence, no nation had previously had the audacity to challenge it in relation to the news media issue. In fact, for a company the size of Facebook, one might think it would take many countries acting in unison to have any impact, in the same way that many countries jointly instituting sanctions against an authoritarian government is often necessary to effect change.

By the 2020s, the leading technology companies had the power to push not only many businesses to success or failure through their platforms, but also governments. This had been recognised by political strategists and analysts following the

Cambridge Analytica affair during the 2016 US presidential election. Facebook shapes contemporary social interactions, friendships, business relationships, intimate relationships, community sentiment and political views. When the industry under threat is the news media in a liberal democracy, there are significant implications, not just for those businesses affected by rapidly declining marketing revenue and their employees (principally journalists), but for the political system itself. If citizens can't obtain objective information about the society they are living in, then they can't effectively exercise their rights within it.[5]

The news media is known as the 'fourth estate', following the three branches of government: the legislative, the executive and the judicial. In 1891, Oscar Wilde commented: 'In old days men had the rack. Now they have the Press. That is an improvement certainly. But still it is very bad, and wrong, and demoralizing … We are dominated by Journalism.'[6] No doubt Wilde's thoughts on social media today would be similarly incisive. Once social media had advanced to the point where it was not just a business but actually had the power to change a nation's culture and politics, and began to cause disquiet in the upper echelons of business, government and the commentariat, regulation became a matter of when, not if.

On the world stage, Australia is best known for its exotic fauna, not for its cultural sophistication or global business leadership. It has a relatively small population, and it's a long way from the centre of global political power. Australian politics rarely makes a ripple in world affairs. If someone from the Northern Hemisphere reads *The Times* or *The Washington Post*, they might know a little about Australian bushfires or floods, or the nation's position on climate change. Otherwise, the last Australian political issue widely discussed in the mainstream media in the United States was possibly the 2017 decision of then deputy prime minister, Barnaby Joyce, to deport actor Johnny Depp's Yorkshire terriers, Pistol and Boo, for breaching biosecurity laws.[7]

One significant policy decision made by Australia is noteworthy in the context of ongoing developments in the US criminal justice system: its gun reforms in the 1990s, specifically a mass buyback of weapons that has helped to maintain a relatively low incidence of gun crime. The reform was prompted by a mass killing at Port Arthur, Tasmania, and is often held up as a model many would like to see implemented in the United States, where a stream of mass shootings continues to take place.[8] Gun crime is still a divisive and troubling issue in the United States, and legislators have not been able to address it effectively. Other policy areas, like Australia's approach to climate change and related international agreements, have been less progressive, probably due to the fact that a major source of the country's wealth has historically come from mining natural resources.

Australia remains closely aligned with the United States, sharing similarities in its language, government and culture, as well as a military and security alliance through the Five Eyes partnership; in fact, the relationship is deepening through new collaborations such as AUKUS. This alliance is likely to become increasingly important over coming decades, due to Australia's position in the Asia–Pacific region and its ongoing strategic and political relationship with the United

States. There are a number of military installations in Australia operated by the United States, such as Pine Gap, in the centre of the continent. The northern city of Darwin is likely to become an important base for potential future US operations in the South China Sea.

As discussed earlier in the book, Australia's geographical proximity to China and its natural resources are also considerations for the United States. China has reduced its trade relationship with Australia in recent years, and both countries have sought alternative markets for many products. This may actually be beneficial for Australia over the long term, in that it reduces the nation's financial dependence on one market, especially since China has shown itself to be willing to use Australia's trade dependencies as leverage in diplomatic disputes. Australia is also well placed to provide the raw materials required to produce new and developing forms of technology, with its reserves of critical 'green' metals.

∞

In both Australia and the United States, news media and particularly newspaper organisations have been significantly impacted by the internet and digitalisation. There has been an explosion in the availability of information, and social media is now the dominant means of information distribution. As people have become accustomed to obtaining free, instant online news, demand for high-quality news journalism has diminished. News media advertising revenue has declined, and many companies have been forced to lay off staff and convert to less profitable (and lower-quality) models. Companies such as Facebook and Google have continued to generate revenue by directing traffic to traditional news sites and hosting news content. Larger news organisations lost revenue, while smaller news organisations – the local town newspaper, in many instances – were decimated or went out of business entirely.

However, the press still holds bargaining power, and they no doubt lobbied politicians in response. While governments around the world were concerned by this trend, as with many areas of technology regulation, they didn't have the will or capacity to address it effectively, and they worried how it might affect them politically, given the influence of the social media companies and their platforms.

It was in this context that Australia took a stand against one of the United States' most powerful technology companies in relation to its use of Australian news media. The Australian government was probably influenced by lobbyists, community sentiment and wider grievances over the disruption caused by technology companies to local businesses. In any case, they tasked their regulatory agencies with developing new laws that would require these companies to pay for the news that was accessible through their websites. This new Australian law would become known as the news media bargaining code.

The technology companies and their lawyers asserted themselves against the Australian government. In January 2021, Google threatened to remove its entire service from the country, preventing Australians from using the dominant internet search engine. This would have affected not just everyday Australians, but businesses that have based their entire revenue on internet traffic. It was untenable in a developed economy like Australia. Google knew it, but gambled that the Australian community would turn against the government and effectively force it to change its position.

Facebook reacted with similar fortitude. In mid-February 2021, it removed all news links from its platform, including the Facebook pages of major news organisations, substantially reducing traffic to the news companies' websites.[9]

Frydenberg immediately criticised these actions and justified the government's approach, saying it 'confirms for all Australians [the] immense market power of these media digital giants'.[10]

The Australian government's position was that news organisations should be compensated for driving traffic to the technology companies' websites. It quoted research findings that found 'out of every $100 Australian dollars spent on advertising in 2019, $53 went to Google, $28 to Facebook, and $19 to all other websites combined, including media outlets'. Others argued that it wasn't the big tech platforms that had ruined the profitability of journalism; rather, it was the free and instantaneous information and opinion available on the internet.[11]

In the end, of course, Facebook and Google did not leave Australia. News content started to reappear nine days later, and the online ecosystem returned to normal. But what had changed was that these platforms were now required to negotiate deals with news organisations to display their news content. Since the new law, Google has implemented more than twenty content agreements with Australian media organisations.[12]

Since 2021, Australia's Digital Platforms Mandatory Bargaining Code has required 'designated' companies negotiate arrangements to compensate the news media companies featured on the digital companies' platforms. None, including Google or Facebook, has actually been designated, because under the code, in deciding whether or not they should be designated, the federal treasurer must consider if there is a marketing imbalance between the digital platform and the Australian news business, and whether the platform has made a contribution to the sustainability of the Australian news industry, such as through arrangements to compensate those businesses for the content.[13]

Google and Facebook have thereby been forced to proactively implement agreements with news companies. This includes all the major Australian organisations, including the Australian Broadcasting Corporation, News Corporation and Seven West Media. The agreements are worth around $200 million per year. They have become a significant revenue stream for the sector, and have increased confidence in Australian journalism. But in 2024, Meta announced it was ending its deals in the latest development of an ongoing battle.[14]

∞

Australia has, to an extent, successfully pushed back against the dominance of these big technology companies, securing a world first in regulation. They prevailed in regulating these companies where others had failed. As you might expect, other countries around the globe were soon looking at the model, and over the next year, Canada, New Zealand, the United Kingdom and the United States were proposing similar codes.[15] It was progressing just as the technology companies had feared: Australia had set a precedent, paving the way for bigger jurisdictions to follow.

It was not the relatively trifling cost of $200 million per year that was of greatest concern to Facebook and Google, but what would happen next. If other liberal democracies introduced similar laws, they knew it was likely that amount would rapidly multiply into billions of dollars annually, and not just in relation to news media. There was also a strong possibility that the approach would likely flow through to other areas of their businesses. It represented the end of an era – the last days of a policy vacuum from which they had benefited as they built themselves into some of the largest companies in the world.

By February 2022, the United Kingdom had developed a similar digital competition bill, and in the United States a journalism competition and preservation bill was drafted. Both followed the Australian approach. The most interesting question is not what the Australian government did to regulate the big technology companies, but how the government achieved it when more-powerful countries around the world were unable to implement similar reforms.

What are the implications for regulation in other technology sectors? Australia is a small country with a small government. Perhaps it can adapt with more agility – although Australians might dispute that characterisation – and organise itself more effectively than the governments of larger nations. Another factor might be that these big technology companies are not headquartered in Australia, and so pay minimal tax. For that reason, the tech giants have less bargaining power than they do when facing off against governments such as that of the United States.

Whatever the reason, Australia is an interesting jurisdiction from the perspective of technology regulation and anyone who uses the internet. Technology regulation is increasingly important for societies everywhere. Understanding how to do it better should be a matter of keen international interest.

∞

To understand this situation – including whether it's a positive development – we need to look at it from the perspectives of those affected. Depending on the nature of the technology regulation issue, each will be more or less relevant. In this case, technical capabilities are not really at the heart of the issue (although they are relevant to Facebook's altering their platform accessibility in response to the government). It is primarily a matter concerning citizens, companies and governments. With regard to the companies themselves, they are the platforms that initially disrupted the news media field. They provide an important service to their users, allowing them to obtain information and communicate with one another in real time, to share images, video, text messages, to discuss their hobbies or their views, and to form or join groups of like-minded people.

From the corporate perspective, conflict between tech companies and the traditional companies that have been disrupted is common across many areas of technology. The platforms are engaging with material available on the internet. What is in dispute is the fair use of that content, and compensation for the creators. The technology companies obtain their profits from advertising and marketing revenue relating to data created by their users. This is highly profitable, and it impacts on the news media companies, which themselves provide a vitally important service: informing the public of what is happening in the world. Due to the tech companies' dominant market share and the vast scale at which they operate, and the consequences if news media companies were to be put out of business, there are compelling reasons for government to step in and ensure that rights and responsibilities align with the public interest.

While individuals have a right to access material that exists on the internet, and it is reasonable that these companies facilitate that, there are also responsibilities in terms of fairness and competitiveness within global and national markets. This is not a purely financial or commercial issue. Broader social and political considerations are highly relevant, especially to the issues we have discussed – the need in liberal democracies for a free and open media, and the provision of information to citizens in order for them to exercise their political capital, hold governments to account and engage in informed debate on public issues. These are the two factors that need to be balanced in this situation: the commercial rights of companies to engage in healthy competition in a free market, and the need to maintain an appropriate range of news media in a liberal democracy.

Smaller governments, such as Australia's, are in a challenging position in relation to these technology companies. They need to regulate large, powerful and influential multinationals that are headquartered in the United States. If the governments achieve their objectives, they will diminish the value of these highly profitable businesses in order to protect their own economies and democracies. This scenario is complicated by the security relationship Australia has with the United States, because of the potential for the political relationship between the countries to be impacted.

Facebook removed many organisations from its platform during its dispute with the Australian government, inconveniencing its users and presumably hoping any related displeasure would be projected onto the government. It was not only news media that was affected, but also community groups and government agencies. It was a risky strategy for the company in terms of its perception in the community.

In mid-2022, Facebook whistleblowers alleged that the company had breached Australia's foreign interference laws by deliberately blocking government agency pages. From a public-relations perspective, the company's approach may have backfired in the longer term. Having failed to sway the Australian government from its intent to regulate them, and while also creating some bad publicity, they may think twice about taking this approach in the future.[16]

∞

The leaders of societies clearly have a right to regulate industries within their jurisdiction. In fact, they have a responsibility to ensure that the functioning of their society is not diminished by technology companies. The strategy adopted by the Australian government in this instance appears to have been effective.

It recognised that the companies have a responsibility to pay for the content they were providing to their users, and from which they were profiting. Facebook clearly wasn't prepared to appropriately compensate those who created the content, so they needed the encouragement of sanctions.

The fact that the Australian government's approach has now been followed by other major economies (including the United States and the United Kingdom) is a sign of its effectiveness. The question is not whether these governments should act in a similar manner, but whether they should have acted sooner and been more proactive, in order to prevent people working in the sector from suffering reduced employment opportunities over the past decade. It's possible that a generation of future journalists has been discouraged from entering the field due to the diminished job prospects.

The potential threat to liberal democracy meant that the issue of news media regulation was especially pertinent. But there is no reason why it couldn't serve as a model for technology regulation in other fields where disruption has impacted employment prospects and consumer choice. Should a similar approach be taken in relation to the disruption of the taxi industry by ride-sharing applications like Uber, for instance? [17] Or is that a field where it is more appropriate for the free market to be left alone, and for consumers to decide which services and companies they find most suitable to their needs? However, ride-sharing applications aren't drawing on the resources of the taxi sector to provide their service; they are providing a new and more efficient service altogether. There was no impact on liberal democracy, although there was an impact on the national interest, with profits flowing offshore rather than staying in local communities. In other areas of technology regulation, more input from technologists to advise on the capabilities of the technology and whether a technology-based regulatory approach could be effective, might be required. In this case, it wasn't required – the law and economics was sufficient.

Leading social media platforms offer a clear example of how multinational tech companies have disrupted traditional businesses and governments. This, of course, is in addition to their power to shape trends and social change in relation to information. As we will see in the next chapter, blockchain technologies have disrupted traditional financial institutions, professional service providers and regulatory agencies, changing the way we purchase, transact and invest.

9. Building with Blocks

Blockchain Infrastructure

Sam Bankman-Fried, otherwise known as SBF, has been a prominent figure of the cryptocurrency sector in the early 2020s. After growing up in California, the son of two law professors, he moved to Boston to attend the Massachusetts Institute of Technology, where he graduated in 2014 with a degree in physics and mathematics. The following eight years would be a wild ride.

Following graduation, Bankman-Fried took a position with the prestigious Jane Street Capital, a Wall Street trading firm undertaking global equities trades of more than US$10 billion a day. He enjoyed working as a trader but had bigger aspirations. After working at the firm for three years, he moved back to California, where he spent a few months at the Centre for Effective Altruism in Berkeley. In 2017 he founded a trading firm of his own, Alameda Research, which specialised in cryptocurrency investments.[1]

A couple of years later, in 2019, Bankman-Fried founded the cryptocurrency derivatives exchange FTX, and from there his financial interests, his investments and his life became increasingly complex, first exploding and then imploding. The business was initially a raging success, especially after the price of cryptocurrency boomed in 2021 and venture capital firms began to invest heavily. At the start of 2022 he was listed as the sixtieth-richest person in the world, with a net worth of US$26 billion.[2] However, by the end of that year he had been arrested for his business activities and his net worth was zero, so to say that he had a bad year would be an understatement. In December 2022, he was facing indictments for wire fraud, commodities fraud, securities fraud, money-laundering and campaign finance law violations; in March 2024 he was sentenced to twenty-five years in prison.[3]

A cryptocurrency exchange (also known as a digital currency exchange, or DCE) is a blockchain platform that enables its customers to trade cryptocurrencies for other cryptocurrencies, or for regular money. In late 2022, when FTX filed for bankruptcy, it was the third-largest exchange in the world, holding approximately US$20 billion in assets. Millions of customers were affected by its collapse, along with institutional investors, other cryptocurrency firms and the general cryptocurrency market. A large amount of FTX customer funds had been loaned to Alameda, and when there was a rapid drop in the value of its digital token, known as FTT, it could not cover its losses when a large number of FTX customers sought to withdraw their funds.[4]

Headlined by the collapse of FTX, the value of cryptocurrency dropped by three-quarters over the course of 2022, which has been described as 'the year crypto came crashing down to Earth'.[5] The FTX case has led to a focus on improving the regulation for cryptocurrency in the United States, with both the Securities and Exchange Commission (SEC) and the US Congress initiating reviews that will influence the sector in the years ahead.[6]

∞

Early versions of cryptocurrencies began to appear in the 2000s, but it was not until 2008, when a person with the apparent pseudonym Satoshi Nakamoto published a paper called 'Bitcoin – A Peer to Peer Electronic Cash System', that it started to become established. The true identity of the person or persons who developed Bitcoin has never been revealed. At around this time, Bitcoin was made available to the public, and the mining process to record and verify transactions commenced.

In the early days Bitcoin wasn't traded – it was actually difficult to assign monetary value to it at all. There is folklore that, during 2010, someone exchanged 10,000 Bitcoin for two pizzas – today that amount of Bitcoin would be worth hundreds of millions of dollars. By 2013, one Bitcoin was valued at approximately $1000. Despite significant fluctuations over the past decade, in early 2023 one Bitcoin was worth around $42,000. These ongoing fluctuations in price, due to several high-profile scams and thefts over the years, have given it a reputation for volatility. But despite this, Bitcoin has become more mainstream and widely accepted as time has gone on – the cryptocurrency market capitalisation is estimated to be about US$3 trillion.[7]

Since Bitcoin was developed, other cryptocurrencies, such as Ether, have also become accepted and widely used. Although cryptocurrency is a controversial field that has been associated with fraud, criminal enterprise, money laundering and charlatans, many have had sustained success and influence without any association with criminality.

One of the most prominent in that category is Vitalik Buterin, a Russian-born Canadian who dropped out of the University of Waterloo to start Ethereum, a blockchain technology software platform with a cryptocurrency known as Ether. Since its founding in 2015, Ether has grown to become the second-largest cryptocurrency by market value behind Bitcoin. The platform is broader than other virtual payment systems, and its blockchain system also supports smart contracts, allowing it to facilitate decentralised transactions. Ethereum is described as an open-source platform where people can 'write code that controls digital value'.[8]

While cryptocurrencies were the first blockchain technology to become mainstream, smart contracts are another application that will likely become just as important. These technology-based contracts are automatically executed by embedding code in a blockchain platform to implement an agreement. They stand in contrast with the traditional approach, which involves having a contract drafted by a lawyer. Under that system, if contractual terms are breached, the law is retrospectively enforced and damages awarded by a court, all of which takes time and money from both parties. Ethereum is the most widely used blockchain platform for smart contracts, using its peer-to-peer network to validate the contractual conditions.[9] Contracts can be automatically executed, including transfer of payments, storage of records and even complex multi-party agreements, such as loan financing and the distribution of company shares or dividends.[10]

Buterin is known as being the most successful Thiel Fellow. These fellowships are awarded by Peter Thiel, a central player in Silicon Valley who founded PayPal and was the first outside investor in Facebook. Thiel now runs the data-analytics company Palantir Technologies and has been an influential figure for many years. His fellowship funds promising young entrepreneurs with $100,000 over a two-year period if they drop out of college and start their own venture. The Thiel Fellowships were described by former Harvard president Larry Summers as 'meretricious' and 'the single most misdirected bit of philanthropy' of the 2010s.[11] Despite pejorative opinions like this, the fellows benefit from mentoring by leaders within a network of scientists, financiers and tech entrepreneurs.

Thiel has long argued that many young people undertake a university degree because it is expected or widely viewed as a worthwhile pursuit, or because they don't know what else to do with their life, but that it often fails to provide a commensurate return on investment. Instead, Thiel advocates the 'need for more thoughtful and personalized approaches to finding success', and his fellowships support those who are talented and prepared to take a different pathway.[12]

∞

As the name suggests, a blockchain can be thought of as a long chain of blocks. All the information within each block is added to those that are newly created in the network, so an identical copy of the blockchain is distributed throughout. It is validated by automated programs that reach consensus on the validity of the information associated with each transaction. Transactions are connected together, each one forming part of the chain. This ensures that there is a record of every transaction that has ever occurred, and that it is transparent, having the form of a public ledger. Cryptography is used to verify and secure the data using mathematical algorithms that protect the integrity of the system. Bitcoin transactions are verified by other users in a process of verifying and confirming transactions called 'mining'. Because complex codes must be solved in order to confirm transactions and ensure the system is not corrupted, 'miners' are needed to process them – in return, they are paid in new Bitcoins.[13]

Despite the volatility that occurred in 2022, blockchain is becoming increasingly important in the global economy. It can potentially improve social inequality and create economic growth through its capacity to decentralise economies, enabling transactions between individuals across the world, without requiring banks, lawyers or accountants. The internet facilitated greater access to information and social connectedness, and blockchain is having a similar impact in the fields of business and finance. The COVID-19 pandemic accelerated the adoption of blockchain technology, which in many places necessitated online transactions due to government-mandated lockdowns. Much like the internet, blockchain technologies reduce the significance of physical and legal boundaries, increasing competition among businesses.

Blockchain has the potential to reshape financial services by reducing transaction costs, settlement time and regulation, although the FTX affair highlighted the risks that are associated with it. Alongside their potential benefits, cryptocurrencies have created new regulatory problems and opportunities for crime. In 2014, for example, a Bitcoin trading exchange called Mt. Gox collapsed when hackers stole US$460 million worth of cryptocurrency; the head of the exchange was convicted of data manipulation in Japan.[14]

Blockchain also has an important role as a form of technology-based regulation, applying code and system architecture to prevent people from cheating on agreements or stealing. Traditionally, approaches to regulation have been reactive, such as legislation that outlaws certain activities, or litigation in the courts. These approaches are retrospective and costly. By contrast, blockchain is cheap and efficient to administer, regulating through technology system design. Because blockchain platforms like Bitcoin and Ethereum are decentralised autonomous organisations, ownership and decision-making is shared among members, rather than being dictated by a government.

In the longer term, further law will be needed to complement blockchain as a form of technology-based regulation. Government must find a way for them to operate harmoniously with technology developments. Regulating blockchain is necessary to ensure stable financial markets and the collection of taxation to fund services and infrastructure, while at the same time enabling the community to benefit from the efficiencies and economic opportunities it can provide. Blockchain will be used across an even wider range of contexts in the future, most likely in the area of data security and infrastructure management.

∞

Cryptocurrency has been a disruptive technology in the global financial sector. It presents challenges for regulators, including from the perspectives of tax evasion, fraud and money laundering. It has also been widely associated with criminal activity: Bitcoin indirectly facilitated the underground website Silk Road, which enabled illicit drugs and other goods and services to be bought and sold with impunity for many years.

In 2011, Ross William Ulbricht, otherwise known as 'Dread Pirate Roberts', founded Silk Road with libertarian ideals, but he also made a lot of money. While users could already obscure their online identity using the Tor browser and virtual private networks (VPNs), it was very difficult to exchange payment for goods or services without identifying themselves. Bitcoin solved this problem, as it did not require a bank account or personal identification to set up an address; all that was needed was an anonymous post office box. Ulbricht provided the rest – for a fee. It was a massive business until he was arrested by the FBI in 2013, by which time the site had made hundreds of millions of dollars in sales.[15]

Digital currencies continue to be associated with crime, due to factors like anonymity, low cost and the way the currency can be rapidly transferred around the world. Some of the scams they have been associated with include Ponzi schemes, market manipulation, money laundering and sanction evasion. The extent of the anonymity they afford is debatable. Law-enforcement agencies can link transactions to real-life identities via cryptocurrency exchanges if they require customers to provide identification documents through 'know your customer' regulations. However, many are located in jurisdictions around the world with less rigorous laws and governance.[16]

While the FTX case has received a great deal of attention, many of the frauds associated with cryptocurrencies are not generally known. Law-enforcement agencies are continually focusing more resources on the detection of financial crimes committed using cryptocurrencies as they become more mainstream. Australian laws were changed to regulate cryptocurrency exchanges in 2017, requiring them to conduct due diligence.[17] As cryptocurrencies become even more widely used in the future, along with other blockchain technology such as smart contracts, effective legislation and better technology measures will be necessary.

As we will see, blockchain itself is likely to facilitate major changes to the way regulation is undertaken.

∞

Blockchain has a myriad of potential applications and will have a major influence on many areas of society in the decades ahead. It can be used to record ownership of intangible products; it has great potential in data protection, as a solution to the current exploitation of vulnerabilities by hackers; and it can be used in a range of other contexts, such as in recording and safeguarding votes in an election. The use of blockchain to record ownership of intangible products will become more important as human interaction increasingly moves into digital realms.

In 2021, Facebook rebranded to become Meta Platforms, a sign of its commitment to the development of a 'metaverse', and of its view that this would be an important part of society and the digital economy in the years ahead. This hasn't come to fruition yet – Meta lost over US$10 billion in the first year, and in 2023 decided to pivot its focus to artificial intelligence. It may have been too early for the metaverse. From a capability perspective, it has been suggested that a 1000-fold increase in computing efficiency would be necessary to support a large-scale movement of people into a metaverse. But eventually it will probably happen: although the metaverse is yet to be widely adopted, or even understood, Meta's investment will likely pay off in the long run.[18]

Interacting in environments that resemble a video game – with 3D virtual worlds, avatars and virtual-reality headsets – is something we will encounter more frequently in the future, for better or worse. Blockchain will be vital to transacting in the metaverse. To buy things, you will need cryptocurrency. Ownership of assets will be tracked on a blockchain, and one way to provide a certificate of authenticity for ownership of a digital asset is with non-fungible tokens (NFTs).

NFTs are unique identifiers, meaning they can't be copied or subdivided, and they can be used to certify authenticity by recording it on a blockchain. Fungibility is a property of a commodity where individual units are interchangeable, and no part can be distinguished from any other part – not the case with NFTs, which are *non*-fungible. They are already being used to refer to proof of ownership of digital files such as an image or video. Digital art is one of the most common use cases of NFTs. In 2021, an NFT of Twitter founder Jack Dorsey's first tweet was sold for US$2.9 million; a picture of the Shiba Inu dog that features on the Doge meme, was sold for US$4 million.[19]

There are many other possible applications of blockchain technology. One useful example that illustrates its potential is voting systems. There are two aspects of distributed ledger technology that are highly relevant to this. The first is that there would be a transparent public record of all votes placed during an election that could help guard against fraud, and the blockchain itself would be highly secure and improve the robustness of the vote. Applying blockchain applications to data security has the potential to solve one of the most significant problems of the current age – how to increase data security and protect information from hackers. This is an ongoing problem for individuals and governments, as data volumes continue to grow exponentially.

∞

As we saw in Chapter 4, governments are establishing national blockchains to support smart contracts and digital currencies – a move that is likely to increase confidence in these platforms for businesses and individuals. Eventually, it is expected that blockchain will become a standard option for almost all transactions. The United States has announced its support for the integration of blockchain into the broader financial system, while in the United Kingdom the government has highlighted the advantages that blockchain can provide in public administration and advocated for its broad adoption in both the public and private sectors.[20]

China is well advanced in this field of technology regulation, already implementing a national blockchain platform. But before these systems become the status quo, there are significant issues that must be worked through. These include governance, security, integration with the broader financial system and contract enforceability. China has proactively adopted many new technologies on a population-wide scale. After previously banning the technology, it is now embracing it.[21]

There are two types of blockchain technology: permissioned and permissionless. In contrast with permissionless blockchain – of which cryptocurrencies like Bitcoin and Ether are examples – permissioned blockchains are not anonymous and so are more tightly regulated. 'Know your customer' (KYC) regulations will encourage governments to move towards permissioned blockchains in the future. For the moment, permissionless blockchains can facilitate the conversion of illicit funds into cryptocurrencies, and smart contracts can automate and complicate transactions, just as shell companies, layers of documentation and tax havens have been used in the past to hide illicit activities. By contrast, in a permissioned blockchain framework all the attributes 'are formulated by the owner, and users are required to seek approval from the application owner before they are able to use the application'.[22]

Interoperability with permissionless blockchain will be a major issue for liberal democracies, where both forms of platform will likely be available. As smart contracts become more widely used, there will need to be greater clarification of legal responsibility when disputes arise due to contractual breaches, and of who will be responsible if the system fails. Because smart contracts are set up by computer programmers, rather than by lawyers and accountants, to what extent those professionals will be involved will need to be worked through. Most likely their influence will be reduced.[23]

∞

As China is an early adopter of new technologies, developments taking place there provide an insight into potential future developments elsewhere. With its authoritarian government, however, they will not be implemented in the same way as in liberal democracies. China's Blockchain-based Service Network (BSN) has already been developed and stands as a world-leading example of this type of national infrastructure. It has been implemented in anticipation of a future in which all information networks are likely to incorporate blockchain technology, providing a platform for a wide range of future technologies, as well as data security.

In the opinion of the Hong Kong–based investor Michael Sung:

[B]lockchain infrastructure would feed other widely promoted efforts to build a 'smart' society through smart cities, connecting encrypted databases linked by 5G to scalable cloud and data management infrastructure in a way that is framed as not feasible with the current decentralised and insufficiently secure systems. The BSN's permissioned blockchain ecosystem ... is imagined to become the key 'infrastructure-of-infrastructures' allowing the vertical integration of cloud computing, 5G communications, industrial internet-of-things (IoT), artificial intelligence (AI), and big data, with fintech and other application-level services on top of the stack.[24]

As the BSN is a permissioned framework, users will be identified and approved before they join, and it will therefore not have anonymity. In fact, it could furnish China's government with even greater oversight and control of private transactions than it has at present. National permissioned blockchain infrastructures in liberal democracies could also increase government control of systems regulating private transactions on the network. Technology-based regulation would allow authorities to simply stop the transaction from proceeding if it does not comply with regulations, rather than retrospectively fining or prosecuting individuals or companies. The parties and the conditions of the contract would be clearly identifiable to regulators, so blockchains that violate the terms of the application and other laws could simply be voided.[25]

Democratic countries have also made progress towards national blockchain infrastructure but are less advanced than China. One example is an Australian national blockchain being developed for the nation's public and private sectors; it will initially be used to exchange and manage smart contracts.[26] There will be an adjustment process over the next twenty years, as companies and individuals begin to accept this as a standard method of contracting. The concept of transacting on a permissioned network will take some time for businesses to accept. Greater efficiency and lower transaction costs will provide an incentive, but there will still need to be accompanying regulation. National blockchain systems will have to be interoperable within international systems, and governments around the world will have to collaborate.

At this stage, blockchain technology is still in its relative infancy. Cryptocurrency has had a big impact in the financial sector, and although it is still associated with risk, it is becoming more widely accepted both as a legitimate payment method and as an investment. Its impact has been uneven: for some it has created rapid and vast wealth, while for others it has been financially ruinous. As in many other areas of new technology, the regulation of cryptocurrency is still catching up. This has provided opportunities for early adopters but also for criminals, who either defraud the unsophisticated or launder the proceeds of their activities.

Smart contracts are yet to have the impact of cryptocurrencies, but they are similarly deregulating professional services, opening up business opportunities and allowing individuals to enter into transactions and take advantage of opportunities that may otherwise be impossible – particularly for those who are not wealthy, or who don't have the resources of a large company.

∞

As we have seen, blockchain technologies are now a major area of technology development, with a growing impact on society. They have changed the way people interact, contract with and relate to one another in their everyday life and in business. All these promise to increase efficiencies, amplify human knowledge and capability, and expand opportunities for collaboration to a broader range of people around the world than has ever before been possible.

Bankman-Fried and his cryptocurrency exchange demonstrated how vast amounts of money can be won and lost on the back of cryptocurrency investment. Volatility and unpredictability are common in the development and application of new technologies such as blockchain. There is initially both high reward and high risk within a lax regulatory environment. In this area of technology, instead of privacy, autonomy and dignity potentially being compromised, the impact can be more directly quantified in financial terms.

Blockchain and cryptocurrency have great potential to improve our lives and provide access to services and business opportunities that may not otherwise have been available. But if they're not regulated appropriately, they can cause great harm, eroding the economy and ruining lives. On the other hand, governments must be careful not to disincentivise innovation. This delicate balance needs to be managed carefully.

Smart contracts can make business agreements more efficient, and can open up business opportunities with international partners that would not otherwise have been possible. They will have an increasing influence in the future, across both the private and public sectors, as more digital infrastructure is developed. Because blockchain platforms can give governments more control over the transactions of citizens and companies, how they are designed – permissioned or permissionless – will play an important role in shaping the future relationship between citizens and the government. This is a question we need to consider now, because effective regulation takes time to develop. In fact, despite the internet being widely used for thirty years, it still isn't effectively regulated. In the next chapter, we will see the European government's attempts to change that.

10. Continental Style

Internet Services

Europe has become a challenging jurisdiction for the United States–based internet companies. For example, as discussed in Chapter 6, Facebook introduced a facial-recognition feature within its systems in 2010 that automatically identified people in photos posted by users and suggested 'tagging' them. In 2012, Facebook turned the feature off for all European accounts in response to concerns from EU regulators and privacy advocates. It also deleted all related data, such as facial-recognition templates, at the request of the Irish data-protection commissioner. In 2018, it brought the feature back as an option, giving European users the opportunity to either block or allow facial recognition on their account.[1]

Nearly four years later, in 2021, Facebook ceased using facial recognition worldwide, deleting the templates of its billion-plus users. By this time, there was global public debate on the use of facial recognition, and a growing number of lawsuits, including in the United States. The company stated at that time: 'We need to weigh the positive use cases for facial recognition against growing societal concerns, especially as regulators have yet to provide clear rules.'[2] In this instance, the progressive regulatory approach in Europe was a harbinger of future international developments.

In 2023, Facebook's parent company, Meta, was fined US$1.3 billion by the European Union for data privacy law breaches relating to the transfer of personal data of European Facebook users to the company's servers in the United States.[3] It had breached Europe's strict requirements relating to the transfer of personal data offshore. The chair of the European Data Protection Board described the actions of the company as serious, noting that the 'transfers are systematic, repetitive and continuous'.[4] The fine was proportionate to the number of European users affected and intended to send a strong signal.[5] Meta paid the fine, but countered that transferring data across borders is fundamental to how the internet works, and that Facebook is relied on by thousands of businesses and other organisations 'in order to operate and provide services that people use every day'.[6] So much of society has now moved online, and the European Union is an important place to observe the approaches that have been applied to controlling it.

The Danish politician Margrethe Vestager serves as the executive vice president of the European Commission for a Europe Fit for the Digital Age. Among other things, she has been described as 'Silicon Valley's most prominent antagonist', and by Donald Trump as 'the tax lady who hates the US'.[7] She continues to play a leading role in Europe's regulation of the internet. Her position is not unreasonable: 'If you offer your services in Europe, there is a European rulebook. And you should live by it. Otherwise, we have the penalties. We have the fines. We have all the assessments and all the decisions that will then come to haunt you.'[8]

Europe has probably been the most important jurisdiction globally in internet regulation to date, and it can't be overlooked. Vestager and the European Union are not content to stop with the billions in fines it has already handed out to technology companies. In 2022, it unveiled several new regulations for internet and technology companies. Negotiations are continuing on a European Union–United States data transfer framework that will integrate new privacy safeguards against intelligence gathering.[9]

Europe is pushing ahead with further reforms. Since the mid-2000s it has been innovative and progressive in responding to many of the societal issues created by the internet, despite what are often complex challenges. Before we get to those reforms, we should look at some examples of how Europe has addressed issues such as privacy, data protection, copyright and freedom of expression.

∞

In 2010, Mario Costeja González filed a claim with the Spanish Authority for Personal Data Protection against the Catalonian newspaper *La Vanguardia* and Google. The claims related to a historical document about him that could be viewed on the internet if anyone searched for his name. It concerned an incident some years earlier, in 1998, when González ran into financial difficulties and a confiscation order was made over his house; it was auctioned by the government to cover a large social security debt.[10] Twelve years later, in 2010, the financial matter with the government had long been resolved; González had moved on and his life was going well. But he was concerned that there was a record of his house being repossessed on the internet that would show up in a Google search, and that this might harm his business interests and reputation. In his words: 'I was fighting for the elimination of data that adversely affects people's honour and dignity and exposes their private lives. Everything that undermines human beings; that's not freedom of expression.'[11]

González's claim to the data-protection agency included two requests: first, that *La Vanguardia* erase his name from its online publication; and second, that Google remove his personal data from the search results it provided to its users. The essence of his claim was that, more than a decade later, the details of his past financial difficulties were irrelevant to the public interest and would only serve to harm him. In the first instance, the Spanish Authority for Personal Data Protection made the decision that the newspaper was not required to take down its publication, because it had been lawfully published. However, it did find that Google, as a personal data processor, should remove the data from its index of search results.[12]

Google appealed, and the matter was referred to the High

Court of Spain, which in turn referred it to the Court of Justice of the European Union, seeking a decision under European law. It too found against Google, on the basis that, as a search engine, it collected data, recorded and organised it in its index programs, stored it on its servers and presented it in search results – controlling the data through these actions. The court weighed the rights of the company to process personal data of this type with González's human rights, specifically his privacy. It found that Google was required to remove the data because it was 'no longer relevant, [and] excessive in relation to the purposes of the processing carried out by the operator of the search engine'.[13]

European law was moving away from viewing search engines like Google as simply intermediaries, and towards stronger regulation of internet companies. The finding of the Court of Justice caused debate as to whether this amounted to a form of censorship. It was attacked by newspapers and media organisations, and hundreds of thousands of requests were directed to Google, seeking to delist internet sites.[14] González's case was decided on the basis of a 1995 regulation called the Data Protection Directive, and became known as the 'right to be forgotten' case.

Europe's progressive regulation of technology companies continued over the next decade. In a later case, the French National Commission on Informatics and Liberty brought an action against Google.[15] The commission wanted to clarify whether Google was required to remove search listings that contained false or damaging information about a person, not just in Europe but globally. This was because Google had introduced a geoblocking mechanism that prevented European users from accessing delisted links, but the data could still be accessed outside Europe.

This time, the court found in favour of Google: it did not have to apply the right to be forgotten globally. '[C]urrently, there is no obligation under EU law, for a search engine operator … to carry out such a de-referencing on all the versions of its search engine,' the court stated.[16]

By the time of that case, which was brought in 2019, the law had been superseded by a new European approach introduced in response to the explosion of personal data that had been stored and uploaded to the internet over the previous twenty years. The new law incorporated the right to be forgotten and a range of other principles seeking to balance individual and organisational rights in the new age of information technology and global business.[17] This was the General Data Protection Regulation.

The regulation applies to companies not based in Europe if they hold the data of EU citizens – and so is obviously relevant to internet and technology companies. It establishes a number of key rights for its citizens, including:

- that data must only be collected if it is necessary;
- the need for clear consent;
- the erasure of data where it is no longer necessary for the purpose it was collected;
- the right to rectify inaccurate personal data;
- the right to transfer personal data to another provider;
- the right not to be subject to a decision based solely on automated processing; and

- the right to be informed when data has been compromised.[18]

Companies that control information must implement technical and organisational measures to ensure that data is held securely, such as encryption. The adequacy of companies' security measures is assessed by taking into account factors like the state of the art, the costs of implementation and the level of risk.[19] It is respected around the world as a leading example of data regulation.

∞

Back in 2003, three young Swedish men decided to create a website. Peter Sunde, Fredrik Neij and Gottfrid Svartholm developed what would become one of the world's most widely used file-sharing resources: The Pirate Bay.

A major issue created by the internet and online technologies is an explosion of copyright infringement. The combination of the internet and the shift from physical forms of data storage (videotapes, cassette tapes, DVDs, CDs) to entirely digital forms facilitated the sharing of creative content like music and films between consumers, and made it easier to evade copyright laws. There have since been many file-sharing sites, including in Europe, but The Pirate Bay has proven resilient and popular over the years.

Since it was started, The Pirate Bay has consistently been one of the most visited sites on the internet. It entered the top 100 within five years, and ten years later still has tens of millions of users. In April 2009, following a trial in a Swedish court, the founders were each sentenced to a year in jail and fined €35 million for facilitating the violation of copyright law through their website. Following an appeal, they were retried in 2010 and given shorter prison sentences.[20]

Internet service providers are required to block their customers from accessing The Pirate Bay in many countries around the world, including in Europe. In 2017, the European Court of Justice considered a case brought by a Dutch copyright holders' group to try to have the website blocked.[21] The Pirate Bay argued that it should be protected by 'safe harbour' provisions that apply to websites such as YouTube, which mean that the sites aren't immediately liable for content that their users upload. However, the court found that the platform 'plays an essential role in making those works available' and has the 'intention of making protected works available to users'.[22]

Copyright is an intellectual property right that protects creative works such as books, musical compositions and films. It doesn't require registration but can be very valuable – some films generate hundreds of millions of dollars. But a new film requires investment of millions of dollars to pay the actors, designers and writers, and it is the law protecting copyright that encourages that investment. Where they can, the studios that own the copyright defend their work against unauthorised copying.[23]

Digital storage technologies and the network capabilities of the internet have radically impacted the entertainment industry by directly facilitating peer-to-peer (P2P) distribution of content worldwide. In the late 1990s, file-sharing sites such as Napster emerged in the United States; it was shut down in just two years.[24] These sites don't actually host the video or audio files, or even link to those files; rather, they host 'tracker' files, which connect users of 'bit torrent' apps to one another, in order for them to download the files from one another directly.

Initially, legal action was taken against the operators of file-sharing services for contributing to the copyright infringement of their users, but when those websites were taken down, new ones were quickly established. Over time, new applications were developed with more distributed storage and sharing mechanisms.[25] Bit torrent technology enabled files to be decentralised and stored in fragments across user networks, then reassembled as complete copies at users' requests.

Until recently, the 'safe harbour' provisions in Europe reflected those that were introduced in the United States.[26] These provide protections for online service providers in some situations if their users have engaged in copyright infringement, with a notice-and-takedown system. Copyright owners can inform online service providers about infringing material, which can then be taken down.[27]

But in 2019 the European Union introduced a new Copyright Directive. This required companies to make their 'best efforts' to remove the offending content. Key questions raised were feasibility, given the size of the internet; jurisdiction, given the different laws that may be in place where the content is uploaded; and free expression, given that the sharing will likely be done using automated filters. There exists the potential for companies seeking to comply with the law to remove legitimate commentary that, on closer inspection, may not actually be infringing copyright, constraining public debate. In 2021, the

European Court of Justice confirmed that online platforms are not considered responsible for content illegally posted by users unless they actively contribute to making it available.[28]

A continuous battle between the entertainment industry, online pirates, internet users and service providers in this arena has reflected the key themes of internet regulation. Balancing these rights continues to be an issue, but technology-based protection and the shift to an online streaming model through companies such as Netflix and Spotify have provided a new revenue stream for content creators. The new model has been highly successful, changing the way music and film is consumed. It has hundreds of millions of subscribers worldwide and tens of billions of dollars in revenue. However, in 2023, concerns among actors and writers about their compensation from streaming services, as well as the impending use of AI in film and television, led to the biggest strike in forty years.[29]

∞

Technology regulation in Europe can be traced back to its strong approach to human rights law. The European Convention on Human Rights was established in 1950 following World War II. It has played a role in the regulation of the internet in Europe over the past decade, having been used in a number of cases involving internet regulation. It protects a number of freedoms in addition to privacy, including those of expression, life, liberty and association.[30]

The importance of the internet to freedom of expression was recognised in the 2012 case *Yildirim v. Turkey*, in which the

European Court of Human Rights stated that the 'Internet has now become one of the principal means by which individuals exercise their right to freedom of expression and information, providing, as it does, essential tools for participation in activities and discussions concerning political issues and issues of general interest'.[31]

In this case, access to Google Sites – an application that allows people to create their own websites – was blocked entirely by the Turkish government. Ahmet Yildirim, a PhD student, created a site that was considered offensive to the memory of Mustafa Kemal Atatürk, a key historical figure in the country who founded the Turkish republic. In deciding the case in favour of Yildirim, the European Court of Human Rights highlighted several matters it took into account, such as whether there was a compelling societal interest, whether it was a last resort, and whether it was proportionate. The court also took into account 'collateral censorship', because a large number of additional websites were affected.[32]

The court has taken a more nuanced approach to human rights in cases involving mass surveillance by governments.[33] One was related to the Edward Snowden disclosures that we discussed in Chapter 5. The UK government's involvement in those activities was challenged on the basis of the right to privacy and freedom of expression. The case was brought by human rights organisations that work with journalists, lawyers, non-government organisations and others who use the internet to communicate in relation to their sensitive work. They accused the government's security agencies of intercepting the content of their communications over the internet as part of expanded state surveillance capabilities that had been facilitated by the internet, the 'bulk interception of Internet traffic transiting through undersea fiber optic cables landing in the U.K., as well as its access to communications and data intercepted in bulk by the intelligence services of other countries'.[34] After an eight-year legal process, the court finally found that European governments can deploy mass surveillance regimes as long as safeguards are incorporated into law.[35]

∞

More recent developments in Europe are the *Digital Services Act*, the *Digital Markets Act* and the *Artificial Intelligence Act*.[36] The *Digital Services Act*, introduced in 2022, is focused on safe online products, illegal content removal and preventing the distribution of disinformation. It also introduces transparency obligations relating to decisions to remove content, and how advertising is tailored to individuals.

There are nineteen platforms that must comply or face fines of up to 6 per cent of their European revenue. They include Amazon, Apple, Google, Instagram, LinkedIn, TikTok, Wikipedia, YouTube, X and Booking.com. Initial responses to the *Digital Services Act* have ranged from criticism from technology companies that it is unclear, burdensome and focused on US companies,[37] through to commentary in the US press that it is a better model and will shape global internet policy because 'the easiest way for a company to ensure it complies anywhere with a strict, specific and comprehensive code is often to comply with it everywhere'.[38]

The *Digital Markets Act* was introduced at the same time. It is focused on the issue of fairness and market contestability in online business, and has established rules to regulate large online platforms such as search engines, social networks, messaging services and video-sharing platforms. A few online platforms have vast market shares – for example, Microsoft has a 78 per cent share of desktop operating systems, Google has 95 per cent of online search and Meta has 90 per cent of social media[39] – leading to concerns in Europe about the use of market power to stifle competition and prevent new players from competing. Under this law, companies of a certain size have obligations: they can't self-preference, pre-install services or restrict access to data. The Act seeks to promote fair prices and choice in the marketplace.[40]

The European Union has also developed one of the world's first laws to regulate AI, known as the *Artificial Intelligence Act*. It incorporates a set of rules for developing, selling and using AI. The law establishes large fines for breaches by companies based outside the European Union that provide AI systems to European users, including companies such as Google, Amazon and Facebook, which have integrated AI functions into their platforms. The *Artificial Intelligence Act* classifies technologies into four risk categories: minimal, limited, high and unacceptable. In the unacceptable risk category, systems are considered unacceptable if they potentially contravene key values and fundamental rights, such as social scoring by governments and real-time biometrics. Limited risk refers to AI systems like chatbots, while minimal-risk systems are things like online video games and spam filters.

AI systems identified as high risk include AI technology used in areas like transport, education, employment, essential services, law enforcement and elections.[41] They are subject to strict obligations, including risk assessments, mitigation, dataset quality checks, documentation and human oversight requirements.[42] If companies don't comply, those the size of Microsoft could be fined tens of billions of euros.[43]

The development of effective regulation for AI, the internet and other new technologies is a key issue for the world to address over the coming decades. Europe has taken an important first step towards this goal. However, legislation and fines in single jurisdictions won't be sufficient. A more comprehensive approach will be necessary, as we will see in the next chapter.

11. Techno 2.0

Technology Regulation

◯

Most people would be aware of the word 'techno' in the context of electronic music. Techno music is associated with loud, fast, synthesised sounds, a tempo of about 120 beats per minute and a 'four on the floor' pattern: the soundtrack to all-night dance parties. Techno music developed in the 1980s, alongside the computing revolution. Although there was a scene in the United States, where it was first played in Detroit, techno music has long been associated with Germany. It is linked with Berlin in particular, where it took off in the 1990s following the fall of the Berlin Wall, which had divided East and West Germany for almost thirty years.

During the reunification celebrations, illegal dance parties were held in abandoned underground stations, power plants and bunkers. People shared this new type of music, bonding over its exhilarating effect on the body as they celebrated freedom, unification and personal expression across East and West Berlin.[1] To this day, Berlin has remained the global centre of techno music. World-famous clubs like Tresor and Berghain, which began as illegal dance parties, were developed into successful businesses, open all night and all weekend.

The techno music range of 100 to 130 beats per minute is also the average rate of a human heart during light exercise. There is an interesting phenomenon where dancing or even listening to this music with others causes heartbeats to synchronise, physically unifying them in a way that otherwise would not seem possible. Techno demonstrates how music can overcome differences between individuals through common experience. This effect is heightened by the release of neurotransmitters and hormones, creating emotional changes in addition to increased and synchronised heart rates.

The spirit of the early techno music scene, with its capacity to bond and bring people together, was maintained as its popularity expanded around the globe. In countries throughout the world there are still vibrant club scenes and underground raves held at abandoned warehouses or remote outdoor locations. Techno, perhaps more than any other form of music, has the power to resonate, encourage social cohesion and promote relationships.[2] While many forms of music have some physiological effect, there are none that do so more than techno.[3] Dancing to techno music at a nightclub or rave enables people to connect through their bodies and shared experience, creating the feeling of being part of something bigger than themselves.

The way techno music can bring people together, promoting synergy and collaboration, reflects the kind of engagement we need if we are to develop effective regulation of new technology. As the previous chapters have demonstrated in a range of fields, many new technologies are developing rapidly and globally, and are associated with complex issues.

There is a lack of effective laws, policies and other measures controlling how new technology is used. This has developed into a major issue for governments, individuals and societies, one that is becoming more complex each year. In most parts of the world, there are more regulations governing the sale of fast food than there are governing AI and other new technologies that will have profound implications on societies. While modern technology has brought benefits, such as more efficient communication, identification and business collaboration, it has also compromised privacy, created inequality, contributed to economic instability and been used to facilitate crime.

Effectively regulating technologies like AI, genomics or blockchain is vital for humanity. We need a better approach to the regulation of technology. Just as techno music creates a resonance between people, we need to find a resonance in technology regulation, in which the key actors are brought together, and their different knowledge and experience harnessed to complement one another, for the benefit of humanity.

We must address this lack of understanding and collaboration. We need a catalyst to bring these groups together, we need an international approach, and we need innovative regulatory strategies. Just as techno music can unite a crowd of people, physically and emotionally, groups of actors relevant to technology regulation must be brought together, practically and intellectually. A resonance between relevant groups of experts and citizens must be found, so that their perspectives can be synthesised into an approach that balances everyone's interests.

Technology regulation is probably the most important public policy issue facing humanity today. As we have seen, the impact of technology on society has been profound and wide-ranging and will only increase. The associated implications for individuals and governments are challenging. Better collaboration is needed among technology experts, individuals, companies and governments, to improve issues like privacy rights and data security while also maintaining the benefits technology can bring.

Technology regulation must take into account everyone's rights and responsibilities and inform regulation that is fair. Different groups of people and entities affected by and involved in technology regulation need to be encouraged to collaborate more coherently in order to maximise the benefits of technology and reduce the potential for harm. Everyone has a position that ought to be considered in the decision-making process of technology regulation, and input is crucial.

Technology regulation is harder and more complex than other forms of regulation. The range of actors is more diverse. It needs to be more responsive and adaptable, because of the tendency for the rapid evolution of technology to outgrow existing laws, and the international implications. *Sui generis* regulation is required – an approach to regulation that is unique to technology.

∞

Through each part of this book, we have discussed many forms of emerging technology, the people behind them, and the associated ethics, law, politics and regulatory issues. Over the past twenty-five years it has been common for new technologies to be adopted before their implications are fully considered and laws made to control their use. This is a feature of the technological revolution we are living through. We need a new approach, providing timely and effective regulation to address these developments.

Technology regulation involves scientific, ethical and legal issues; it needs to be nimble and global. Technologies such as AI, social media and cryptocurrencies have created massive regulatory gaps. They create opportunities and advantages for some and disadvantage for others. Technology may be improving efficiency, providing better access to knowledge and opening up new business opportunities, but it is simultaneously exploiting users' personal data and creating a range of risks and harms. A central aspect of technology regulation is the trade-off between individual rights and the collective needs of society. It is the role of governments to limit the harmful aspects of new technology, while facilitating the development and adoption of its beneficial applications and attributes.

In the preceding chapters, we have seen how the emergence of cryptocurrencies created new opportunities outside the mainstream financial system, but also how it has facilitated criminal activity. We've explored how the global operation of technology companies increases the risk of regulatory gaps. In relation to social media, we saw how, as a consequence of the vast size of multinational technology companies such as

Alphabet and Meta, they have disproportionate influence over individuals, smaller businesses, governments and regulatory agencies. We have seen how AI necessitates new principles of responsibility and liability to be developed and integrated into legal systems.

There are so many new and varied technologies requiring regulation, each used in multiple contexts, and each with multiple unique risks and benefits to be balanced. Past regulation has required cumbersome legislation, policies, standards and procedures across various areas of society and business. There are thousands of governments at state and national levels all over the world, with their own approaches and systems. It is a major challenge to establish coherent, consistent and effective oversight of new technologies.

What we need is a new and multifaceted approach. The new approach needs three aspects. It must bring together the key actors, it must regulate using technology and it must involve a new international agency to coordinate and help governments enforce standards around the world.

∞

The first imperative is *involving the key actors*. In order to determine what laws and technology-based measures are needed, and how they should be structured and integrated, advice is needed. Technology experts and users must be integrated into the process and consulted, in order to balance the rights and responsibilities of those affected.

There are six groups of actors that we need to bring together:

- Scientists, such as engineers, biologists and information technology professionals, who develop technology through their knowledge, training, expertise and innovation, and can provide advice in relation to its capabilities and implementation.
- Companies, which invest in and develop new technology products or services, and then take them to market, serving consumers and generating profits.
- Private citizens, who are the consumers of technologies, or the subjects of technologies managed by companies and governments.
- Ethicists, who analyse and justify the moral reasons for regulation.
- Legal professionals, such as lawyers and judges, who can provide advice to governments and companies on legislation, and resolve disputes that arise.
- Governments, which must coordinate and lead the regulation of technology through legislation and the implementation of technology-based systems to control it.

The rights and responsibilities of all of these actors are interrelated. A company has a duty not only to consumers but also to other companies (not to infringe their intellectual property) and to governments (to pay tax and follow consumer and labour laws). Scientists have a responsibility to act professionally and uphold their collective reputation beyond the financial objectives of their role within the company that employs them, and must also consider factors such as the safety of consumers. Private citizens, while having a right to expect that companies are selling technology that is safe and will not harm them, also have a responsibility to use technology in a manner that does not harm other citizens and that complies with criminal and other laws. Governments have a responsibility to make laws that protect their citizens from the possible harms caused by technology, but they also have a responsibility to use technology in a way that does not disregard or exploit the human rights of their citizens, and to establish economic policies that encourage and reward innovation.[4]

Take electric vehicles as an example. The manufacturer is reliant on research, development, implementation and advice from scientists and engineers, on other companies to provide components, and on governments to register their cars for use and to build roads. Without computer hardware, AI systems, GPS satellites, lightweight but powerful batteries, and the basic road infrastructure provided by governments, electric vehicle companies could not develop and offer a valuable product to their customers. If an electric vehicle has not been tested and registered by a government that allows it to be driven on its roads, it has little value to a consumer – or, consequently, to a company, if it cannot profit from its sale.

Individuals and societies gain benefits from electric car technology, in the form of cheaper, cleaner, more efficient private transport, but they must also consider how their location and other data collected by sophisticated electric vehicles may impact on their privacy, and how autonomous systems may impact their safety. The company itself must comply with privacy laws and not unreasonably exploit personal data; computer scientists employed by the company are responsible for providing advice and implementing systems to maintain data security and user safety; and state, federal and international governments around the world must collaborate in enacting legislation that regulates a company that might be headquartered in the United States but operates in hundreds of different jurisdictions, each with its own legal system.

This is the case for most technologies: without the computers or smartphones produced by manufacturers like Apple, internet companies such as Google could not provide access to information or generate advertising revenue. A smartphone without a connection to a telecommunications network cannot send text messages or receive phone calls, and cannot access social networking applications. It can record video or a picture but not communicate it. Google requires computer scientists to develop and maintain its websites, and on private citizens to upload content and connect with other citizens – and all of it relies on governments to uphold a sufficiently orderly society to enable the economy to function effectively.

More than other areas of public policy, technology regulation must incorporate the perspectives of a complex network of actors, and take into account their rights and responsibilities.

∞

The second imperative is *regulating with technology*. Many of the regulatory challenges presented by new technology can be traced back to the development of the internet. The internet was a massive technological achievement, but its ability to transmit information around the world instantaneously has profound implications. State-based sovereignty and jurisdiction is uniquely challenged by the internet and the subsequent technologies it has facilitated.[5] The internet demonstrated the inadequacy of using only law to regulate and having different laws in place around the world.

The internet necessitated new ideas in technology regulation, including the realisation that laws can be imposed by technological capabilities and system designs, rather than only by proscribing activities with legislation.[6] This concept has evolved over the past twenty-five years and is now being used by governments, such as in requiring internet service providers to block their customers from accessing illegal websites.

Regulation can incorporate law as well as technology system design to control individual behaviour, to operate in both the real world and digital domains. Because it is difficult for traditional laws to control activities that take place online, combining them with technology-based measures is more likely to be effective.[7] Legislation is still needed but is less likely to be effective in isolation.[8]

The advantage of using technology systems for regulation is that it has a higher level of compliance than legislation. At best, a high proportion of the population will not have the technical ability to circumvent it. It proactively prevents noncompliance, rather than deterring by the threat of fines or jail, or by punishing after the fact if a person or company breaks the law. It is also a low-cost, efficient option for governments, because the costs can be borne by the private sector when they build systems that comply with regulatory requirements. But a downside is that, in contrast with enacting laws in the parliament of a liberal democracy, it is less transparent.[9] As blockchain and smart contracts become more established, they will likely play a key role in this type of technology regulation.

∞

The third imperative is to establish a *dedicated international agency* for coordinating technology regulation. AI and other forms of new technology have significant implications for all humanity, and an international approach is needed. It has taken until the mid-2020s, but it seems as though recent developments in AI have raised awareness and provided an impetus for governments to seriously consider establishing specialised agencies to regulate AI and other emerging technologies.

Even the AI industry itself is calling on governments to act. When Sam Altman, the head of one of the most influential AI companies, appeared before the US Congress in May 2023, he told the government that reforms were urgently needed. Senators described it as a historic moment. As one said: 'I can't recall when we've had people representing large corporations or private sector entities come before us and plead with us to regulate them.'[10]

An international regulatory agency could facilitate effective collaboration between governments and the other relevant actors. It would take advice, consider the relevant issues and formulate and enforce the protective measures that companies must incorporate within their systems.[11] This could take the form of a licensing scheme in relation to algorithms and other technologies, with a focus on transparency, risk mitigation, safety and respect for human rights. Licences could be granted for the use of an application in specific contexts according to the level of risk, as Europe is already seeking to do.

Under models that have been proposed, a regulatory agency focused on technology would provide direction to multinational companies in relation to the use of personal data to generate content or make a decision, and require audits or risk assessments to evaluate the harms their tools could potentially cause. This is especially important in relation to companies that are implementing cutting-edge technology.[12] Leading tech companies have enormous resources, and regulatory agencies, if they are to be effective, must have the funding necessary to undertake their work.[13]

An international approach is vital. The actions of large governments such as the United States, China and the European Union will be important, but ultimately they cannot address this issue individually. Governments must collaborate, and this should be led by an international group, perhaps associated with an organisation such as the OECD or the United Nations.

We need a new model for international technology governance. The wide range of examples discussed throughout this book highlight the need for a new approach, one that involves consultation with relevant experts and the individuals affected, one that has the authority to coordinate and compel the implementation of technical and legal solutions around the world. The growing appreciation of the significance of AI will help to produce the necessary impetus for progress, and lead to a new approach being implemented that will facilitate a more positive relationship between humans and technology.

Afterword

Petite Mort

●

Throughout this book we have looked at how technology has driven and shaped this extraordinary era we are living through. We began by considering the need to examine and reflect on the technological revolution: how it is impacting the world today, and how it is likely to do so in the future. In the midst of it, we may not have the perspective to fully appreciate just how much has occurred in such a short period of time, and the implications for humanity. But if we reflect on the technological developments that have occurred throughout history, the extent to which new technologies have changed everyday life in just twenty-five years is amazing.

Technology and its regulation is the defining issue of the time we are living in – we must take it seriously. The complexity of technology companies' products, financial resources and global nature means that national governments must collaborate to achieve effective regulation. Governments have so far not devoted enough resources to addressing the costs of new technology: privacy impacts, crime, social inequality and the potential for artificial general intelligence to change the world in ways we cannot even anticipate. One reason may be that we are so immersed in technology that we haven't thought enough about why it needs to be regulated, and impressed this on our leaders.

New technology has simultaneously empowered and disempowered individuals. We have better access to information and services, but this has led to the data-based business model adopted by a new generation of technology entrepreneurs. Online search has monetised our browsing history to provide more efficient advertising, leading the way for later companies to monetise our faces and our genomes. Law-enforcement agencies taking fingerprints, or evidence from a suspect's phone under warrant, evolved into data systems that record everything done online. What started with uploading a profile photo to a website soon became fodder for surveillance systems, algorithms, deep fakes and disinformation. Personal data is now used as extensively by companies and governments as the state of the art can facilitate; privacy legislation has had little impact.

The internet provided the foundation for a new generation of social technology applications. Social media has connected people and changed the world – to such an extent that it has transformed knowledge dissemination, politics and aspects of liberal democracy. Facebook disrupted news media, advertising and other industries, influenced elections and led an evolution in the dynamics of human relationships. It has never been easier to network, transmit information and reach a target audience.

Now blockchain technology is decentralising and disrupting financial systems and redistributing wealth through cryptocurrency and smart contracts, opening access to a wider range of players. Many more people are now able to transact across the globe, without the expense of lawyers, accountants, bankers, currency exchanges and documentation. New business opportunities abound – but so do opportunities for fraud, as the FTX collapse illustrated.

The discrete technologies required for social credit systems are largely in place around the world, but only one country – China – is openly establishing comprehensive, integrated digital governance. It is likely that similar systems will eventually be implemented in many countries across the globe, potentially changing the fabric of liberal democracy and its values. Entrusting AI with these datasets will furnish it with a great deal of power.

The technology revolution has major implications for governments and international relations. Mineral resource allocation, climate change, the development of even more advanced industries and military applications of technology will affect world politics and the international order. The influence of governments may be diminished as technology and AI inevitably become more sophisticated. The groundbreaking but still traditional approach to technology regulation that Europe has enacted – legislation and fines – is an admirable start, but ultimately this method alone won't be sufficient. Controlling

AI and other technologies will require the collaboration of governments around the world, and will have to incorporate innovative forms of technology-based regulation.

Nineteenth-century philosopher Friedrich Nietzsche is one of the best-known existentialists, who focus on questions associated with the meaning of human life and humans' place in the world. Nietzsche published his works during the 1800s, an important period in human history when a secular world was emerging, and the influence of Christianity was being challenged by a growing awareness of scientific advancements. Discoveries in astronomy, physics and biology were changing our understanding of the world and the universe around us.

Nietzsche's assertion that 'God is dead' comes from this time. He was seeking to highlight that, as a result of human advancements in knowledge during the Enlightenment – fundamental scientific discoveries, alongside the development of more sophisticated ethical and political theories – humans no longer needed religion as a source of value and order in the universe. According to Nietzsche, humans had, to some extent, 'killed' God through their achievement in obtaining a greater understanding of the world.

As well as making a leading contribution to scientific advancement, AI of the future will create art, music, poetry, literature and philosophy. If, despite our best attempts at regulation, AI does overwhelm humans, integrate with the other technologies we have looked at and, through its vastly superior intellectual capacity, gains control of the world, how would a large language model make sense of the world and AI's place in it? It would ingest the writing of the most influential humans that had come before it – including Nietzsche and his widely quoted views on humans' status at a time when science had caused them to reorder their thinking. Might the AI then generate the phrase 'Humans are dead'? Figuratively, that could succinctly encapsulate the diminished relevance of humans in the world. So the pinnacle human achievement may in fact precipitate the cessation of some aspects of it. A contradiction of modern life, but one we will quickly be forced to move on from following a period of brief reflection. We are hardwired to reinvigorate, to continue to pursue human advancement and to evolve.

As religion still has a role in the world today, so too will humans in a world led by superior AI technology. In the future, humans may coexist with AI, just as religion now coexists with science. Although religion cannot explain the physical world in the way science can, it provides an important view that science cannot. Humans, too, will continue to provide a perspective on the world that AI cannot.

At least, let us hope that is the case. Perhaps, due to the inferiority of the human mind in comparison with AI, we won't be making the most important contribution to discussions on issues like climate change, health problems in the developing world, or even technology development and regulation. We simply won't have the nous to participate at the same intellectual level. Instead, humans may simply moderate and relay the conclusions of AI, filtering them through a human lens.

The implications of AI, and the crucial importance of regulating it, are just beginning to enter the public's consciousness. This is bringing greater attention to the need for better regulation of other technologies, which is clearly a related issue. We have looked across the relationship between humans and technology, the impacts on and implications for governments, individuals and society, the importance of effective regulation and how we can begin to achieve it. As we have seen, technology regulation must incorporate institutions that provide the perspectives of all the relevant actors on an ongoing basis. It must also use technology as well as legislation to regulate. Finally, it must stem from international government collaboration and enforcement.

During our lifetimes, establishing the sustainable coexistence of humans and technology will be humanity's most important project. Despite the complex challenges presented by AI and other technologies, we should be optimistic that we can move into a new era of technology advancement, one defined by effective technology regulation.

Notes

Preface

1 Genesis 3:4–5, New International Version, 2011.

1. Techno

1 'Elon Musk signs open letter urging AI labs to pump the brakes', *Time*, 29 March 2023, https://time.com/6266679/musk-ai-open-letter.

2 Hong Cheng et al., 'The Rise of Robots in China', *Journal of Economic Perspectives*, vol. 33, 2019, pp. 71–88.

3 Michael T. Nietzel, 'US universities fall behind China in production of STEM PhDs', *Forbes*, 7 August 2021, www.forbes.com/sites/michaeltnietzel/2021/08/07/us-universities-fall-behind-china-in-production-of-stem-phds.

4 Josh Rogin, 'The most shocking intel leak reveals new Chinese military advances', *The Washington Post*, 13 April 2023, www.washingtonpost.com/opinions/2023/04/13/china-hypersonic-missile-intelligence-leak.

5 Melanie Burton, 'Tesla to buy more than $1 bln of Australian battery minerals a year', *Reuters Business*, 2 June 2021, www.reuters.com/business/sustainable-business/tesla-buy-more-than-1-bln-australian-battery-minerals-year-2021-06-02.

6 AGL Discover, *Six Australian Innovations that Changed the World*, 2021, https://discover.agl.com.au/progress/six-australian-innovations-that-changed-the-world.

7 National Geographic, *Europe: Human Geography*, 2023, https://education.nationalgeographic.org/resource/europe-human-geography.

8   Keil Institute for the World Economy, *Tension within the European Union*, 2023, www.ifw-kiel.de/topics/tension-within-the-european-union.

9   European Union, *The Artificial Intelligence Act 2022*, https://artificialintelligenceact.eu.

2. Means of Production

1   Council on Foreign Relations, *South China Sea Tensions*, 2014, www.cfr.org/backgrounder/south-china-sea-tensions.

2   Ibid.

3   Simone McCarthy, 'Beijing warns of "severe impact" on US–China relations as Taiwan's leader lands in New York', CNN, 30 March 2023, https://edition.cnn.com/2023/03/30/asia/tsai-ing-wen-taiwan-new-york-city-china-response-intl-hnk/index.html.

4   Ibid.

5   Irene Entringer et al., 'What is the likelihood of war over Taiwan?', *Foreign Policy*, 13 April 2023, https://foreignpolicy.com/2023/04/13/china-attack-taiwan-war-expert-poll-biden.

6   Prime Minister of Australia, 'Fact Sheet: Implementation of the Australia–United Kingdom–United States Partnership (AUKUS)', 5 April 2022, https://pmtranscripts.pmc.gov.au/sites/default/files/AUKUS-factsheet.pdf.

7   UNSW, 'Why are submarines so important?', 2021, www.unsw.adfa.edu.au/newsroom/news/ask-expert-why-are-submarines-so-important.

8   United States Environmental Protection Agency, 'Nuclear submarines and aircraft carriers', 2023, www.epa.gov/radtown/nuclear-submarines-and-aircraft-carriers.

9   Paul Dempsey, 'View from Washington: AUKUS looms over AI and quantum', *Engineering & Technology*, 17 September 2021.

10   Ibid.

11   Matt McDonald, 'Securitization and the construction of security', *European Journal of International Relations*, vol. 14, 2008, pp. 563–87.

12   Marcus Smith & Patrick Walsh, 'Improving health security and intelligence capabilities to mitigate biological threats', *International Journal of Intelligence, Security, and Public Affairs*, vol. 23, 2021 pp. 139–55.

13   'Taiwan's dominance of the chip industry makes it more important', *The Economist*, 6 March 2023, www.economist.com/special-report/2023/03/06/taiwans-dominance-of-the-chip-industry-makes-it-more-important.

14   Ibid.

15   Benjamin Yacobi, *Semiconductor Materials: An Introduction to Basic Principles*, Springer, 2003.

16 The law is named after Gordon Moore, the co-founder of Fairchild Semiconductor and Intel, who first described the phenomenon.

17 'Supply chain issues and autos: When will the chip shortage end?', J.P. Morgan, 18 April 2023, www.jpmorgan.com/insights/research/supply-chain-chip-shortage.

18 Ibid.

19 Ibid.

20 Gregory C. Allen, *Choking Off China's Access to the Future of AI*, Centre for Strategic and International Studies, 2022.

21 Ibid.

22 Che-Jen Wang, 'China's semiconductor breakthrough', *The Diplomat*, 20 August 2022.

23 'The most dangerous place on Earth', *The Economist*, 1 May 2021, www.economist.com/leaders/2021/05/01/the-most-dangerous-place-on-earth.

24 Kif Leswing, 'Apple chipmaker TSMC warns Taiwan–China war would make everybody losers', CNBC, 2 August 2022, www.cnbc.com/2022/08/02/apple-chipmaker-tsmc-warns-taiwan-china-war-would-make-everybody-losers.html.

25 United Nations, *Climate Action*, 2023, www.un.org/en/climatechange.

26 Ibid.

27 Ibid.

28 Richard Herrington, 'Mining our green future', *Nature Reviews Materials*, vol. 6, 2021, pp. 456–88.

29 National Archives, 'Remarks of President Barack Obama – Address to Joint Session of Congress', 24 February 2009.

30 Clean Energy Council, *Clean Energy Australia Report 2023*, Melbourne, 2023.

31 'China says a third of electricity will come from renewables by 2025', *Reuters*, 1 June 2022, https://www.reuters.com/business/sustainable-business/china-says-third-electricity-will-come-renewables-by-2025-2022-06-01/.

32 Benjamin Sovacool et al., 'Sustainable minerals and metals for a low-carbon future', *Science*, vol. 367, no. 6473, 2020, pp. 30–33.

33 International Energy Agency, *The Role of Critical Minerals in Clean Energy Transitions*, IEA Publications, 2023.

34 Benjamin Sovacool et al., 'Sustainable minerals and metals for a low-carbon future', *Science*, vol. 367, no. 6473, 2020, pp. 30–33.

35 Minerals Council of Australia, *Australian Mining*, 2023, https://minerals.org.au/wp-content/uploads/2023/01/Advantage-Australia.pdf.

36 Bruce Shen, 'China's dominance over critical minerals faces new challengers', *The Diplomat*, 10 November 2022, https://thediplomat.com/2022/11/chinas-dominance-over-critical-minerals-faces-new-challengers.

37 Colin Stuart, 'A race is afoot to make billions from the moon's resources', BBC, 17 June 2022, www.sciencefocus.com/space/new-space-race-moon.
38 Ibid.
39 European Space Agency, *Helium-3 Mining on the Lunar Surface*, 2022, www. esa.int/Enabling_Support/Preparing_for_the_Future/Space_for_Earth/ Energy/Helium-3_mining_on_the_lunar_surface.
40 United Nations Office for Outer Space Affairs, *Treaty on Principles Governing the Activities of States in the Exploration and Use of Outer Space, including the Moon and Other Celestial Bodies*, 1966, www.unoosa.org/oosa/en/ourwork/ spacelaw/treaties/introouterspacetreaty.html.
41 Colin Stuart, 'A race is afoot to make billions from the moon's resources', BBC, 17 June 2022, www.sciencefocus.com/space/new-space-race-moon.
42 Bruce Reed, *Manhattan Project: The Story of the Century*, Springer, 2022.
43 Kevin Rudd, 'Short of war: How to keep U.S.-Chinese confrontation from ending in calamity', *Foreign Affairs*, 5 February 2021, www. foreignaffairs.com/articles/united-states/2021-02-05/kevin-rudd-usa-chinese-confrontation-short-of-war.
44 *National Security Legislation Amendment (Espionage and Foreign Interference) Act 2018* (Cth).
45 Section 1286.
46 United States Government Department of Education, 'U.S. Department of Education Uncovers Vast Underreporting of Foreign Gifts and Contracts by Higher Education Institutions', 20 October 2020.
47 Kylie Long, et al., 'Rising global fears of foreign interference in higher education', *International Higher Education*, vol. 107, 2021, pp. 8–10.
48 Racqueal Legerwood, 'As US universities close Confucius Institutes, what's next?', *Human Rights Watch Dispatch*, 27 January 2020.
49 Australian Government Department of Education, Skills and Employment, *Guidelines to Counter Foreign Interference in the Australian University Sector*, 2021.
50 United Kingdom Government Centre for the Protection of National Infrastructure, *Trusted Research*, 2022.

3. Rise of the Machines

1 OpenAI, 'Introducing ChatGPT', https://openai.com/blog/chatgpt.
2 Krystal Hu, 'ChatGPT sets record for fastest-growing user base', *Reuters*, 3 February 2023, www.reuters.com/technology/chatgpt-sets-record-fastest-growing-user-base-analyst-note-2023-02-01.
3 IBM, 'What is artificial intelligence', www.ibm.com/topics/artificial-intelligence.
4 Martin Ford, *The Rise of the Robots: Technology and the Threat of Mass Unemployment*, Oneworld, 2015.

5   Marcus Smith & Rachael Heath Jeffery, 'Addressing the challenges of artificial intelligence in medicine', *Internal Medicine Journal*, vol. 50, 2020, pp. 1278–81.

6   Ibid.

7   Neuralink, 2023, https://neuralink.com.

8   Kevin Roose, 'The brilliance and weirdness of ChatGPT', *The New York Times*, 12 May 2023, www.nytimes.com/2022/12/05/technology/chatgpt-ai-twitter.html.

9   Ibid.

10 Ibid.

11 Will Heaven, 'Why GPT-3 is the best and worst of AI right now', *MIT Technology Review*, 24 February 2021, www.technologyreview.com/2021/02/24/1017797/gpt3-best-worst-ai-openai-natural-language.

12 Will Heaven, 'ChatGPT is OpenAI's latest fix for GPT-3. It's slick but still spews nonsense', *MIT Technology Review*, 30 November 2022, www.technologyreview.com/2022/11/30/1063878/openai-still-fixing-gpt3-ai-large-language-model.

13 Ibid.

14 John Koetsier, 'GPT-4 beats 90% of lawyers trying to pass the bar', *Forbes*, 14 March 2023, www.forbes.com/sites/johnkoetsier/2023/03/14/gpt-4-beats-90-of-lawyers-trying-to-pass-the-bar.

15 Alex Hern, 'What is GPT-4 and how does it differ from ChatGPT?', *The Guardian*, 16 March 2023, www.theguardian.com/technology/2023/mar/15/what-is-gpt-4-and-how-does-it-differ-from-chatgpt.

16 Ibid.

17 Babak Bejnordi et al., 'Diagnostic assessment of deep learning algorithms for detection of lymph node metastases in women with breast cancer', *Journal of the American Medical Association*, vol. 318, 2017, pp. 2199–2210.

18 Scott McKinney et al., 'International evaluation of an AI system for breast cancer screening', *Nature*, no. 577, 2020, pp. 89–94.

19 Andrew Esteva et al., 'Dermatologist-level classification of skin cancer with deep neural networks', *Nature*, no. 542, 2017, pp. 115–18.

20 Food and Drug Administration, *Proposed Regulatory Framework for Modifications to Artificial Intelligence/Machine Learning-Based Software as a Medical Device Discussion Paper*, US Government, 2020.

21 Vernor Vinge, 'Technological singularity'. The original version of this article was presented at the VISION-21 Symposium, sponsored by NASA Lewis Research Center, and the Ohio Aerospace Institute, 30–31 March 1993. It appeared in the winter 1993 issue of *Whole Earth Review*. See http://cmm.cenart.gob.mx/delanda/textos/tech_sing.pdf.

22 Ibid.

23 Ibid.
24 Nisha Talagala, 'Don't worry about the AI singularity: The tipping point is already here', *Forbes*, 21 June 2021, www.forbes.com/sites/nishatalagala/2021/06/21/dont-worry-about-the-ai-singularity-the-tipping-point-is-already-here.
25 Ray Kurzweil, *The Singularity Is Near*, Penguin, 2005, p. 30.
26 Rory Cellan-Jones, 'Stephen Hawking warns artificial intelligence could end mankind', BBC News, 2 December 2014, www.bbc.com/news/technology-30290540.
27 Danielle Abril, 'AI isn't yet going to take your job – but you may have to work with it', *The Washington Post*, 20 March 2023, www.washingtonpost.com/technology/interactive/2023/ai-jobs-workplace.
28 Maaten Goos, A. Manning & A. Salomons, 'Explaining job polarization: Routine-biased technological change and offshoring', *American Economic Review*, vol. 104, 2014, pp. 2509–26.
29 James Bessen, 'How computer automation affects occupations: Technology, jobs, and skills', Boston University School of Law & Economics Working Paper No. 15-49, 2015.
30 The White House, *The Impact of Artificial Intelligence on the Future of Workforces in the European Union and the United States of America*, 2022, www.whitehouse.gov/wp-content/uploads/2022/12/TTC-EC-CEA-AI-Report-12052022-1.pdf.
31 Eurostat, 'Digital economy and society statistics – enterprises', *Eurostat Statistics Explained*, 20 January 2022, https://ec.europa.eu/eurostat/statistics-explained/index.php?title=Digital_economy_and_society_statistics_-_enterprises.
32 U.S. Bureau of the Census, 'Annual Business Survey', 2019, www.census.gov/programs-surveys/abs/data/tables.html.
33 OpenAI, 'ChatGPT', 2023, https://openai.com.
34 Ibid.
35 United Nations, *Human Rights*, 2023, www.un.org/en/global-issues/human-rights.
36 Ibid.
37 Organisation for Economic Co-operation and Development, *Recommendation of the Council on Artificial Intelligence*, 2019, https://legalinstruments.oecd.org/en/instruments/OECD-LEGAL-0449.
38 The White House, 'Blueprint for an AI Bill of Rights', 2022, www.whitehouse.gov/ostp/ai-bill-of-rights.
39 Future of Life Institute, 'Pause giant AI experiments: An open letter', 22 March 2023, https://futureoflife.org/open-letter/pause-giant-ai-experiments.
40 Ibid.

41 Marcus Smith & Rachael Heath Jeffery, 'Addressing the challenges of artificial intelligence in medicine', *Internal Medicine Journal*, vol. 50, 2020, pp. 1278–81.

4. Discrete Data Points

1 State Council of the People's Republic of China, 'Planning Outline for the Construction of a Social Credit System', 2014, https://chinacopyrightandmedia.wordpress.com/2014/06/14/planning-outline-for-the-construction-of-a-social-credit-system-2014-2020.

2 Drew Donnelly, 'China social credit system explained – What is it & how does it work?', NH Global Partners, 2023, https://nhglobalpartners.com/china-social-credit-system-explained.

3 Marcus Smith & Gregor Urbas, *Technology Law: Australian and International Perspectives*, Cambridge University Press, 2021.

4 Daithi Sithigh & Mathias Siems, 'The Chinese social credit system: A model for other countries?', *The Modern Law Review*, vol. 82, 2019, pp. 1034–71.

5 Nathan Vanderklippe, 'Chinese blacklist an early glimpse of sweeping new social-credit control', *The Globe and Mail*, 3 January 2018.

6 John Danaher et al., 'Algorithmic governance: Developing a research agenda through the power of collective intelligence', *Big Data & Society*, July–December 2017, pp. 1–21.

7 Alec Ash, '"1984" algorithm to control life in China', *The Times*, 11 June 2017.

8 Joel Reidenberg, 'Lex informatica: The formulation of information policy rules through technology', *Texas Law Review*, vol. 76, 1998, p. 553.

9 Lawrence Lessig, *Code and Other Laws of Cyberspace*, Basic Books, 1999.

10 Marcus Smith, 'A modern approach to regulation: Integrating law, system architecture and blockchain technology in Australia', *Australian Business Law Review*, vol. 48, 2020, pp. 460–66.

11 Clemens Binder, 'Happenings foreseen: Social media and the predictive policing of riots', *Security and Peace*, vol. 34, 2016, 242–47.

12 In Australia, for example, this came into effect in 2015, and since then telecommunications service providers have been required to retain metadata and store it for two years. See *Telecommunications (Interception and Access) Amendment (Data Retention) Act 2015* (Cth).

13 Seumas Miller & Patrick Walsh, 'NSA, Snowden and the ethics and accountability of intelligence gathering', in J. Galliott & J. Reed (eds), *Ethics and the Future of Spying: Technology, Intelligence Collection and National Security*, Routledge, 2016, pp. 193–204.

14 Pat O'Malley & Gavin Smith, '"Smart" crime prevention? Digitization and racialized crime control in a Smart City', *Theoretical Criminology*, vol. 26, no. 1, 2022, pp. 40–56.

15 Ibid. There is a stark overrepresentation of First Nations people in the criminal justice system in Darwin: 84 per cent of the prison population are Indigenous, and as a group they face social-economic inequality.

16 Karen Wong & Amy Dobson, 'We're just data: Exploring China's social credit system in relation to digital platform ratings cultures in Westernised democracies', *Global Media and China*, vol. 4, 2019, pp. 220–32.

5. Back Doors

1   Matt Johnston, '5-eyes giant L3 snaps-up locals Azimuth and Linchpin for $313m', *IT News*, 7 September 2018, www.itnews.com.au/news/5-eyes-giant-l3-snaps-up-locals-azimuth-and-linchpin-for-313m-512203.

2   Lorenzo Franceschi-Bicchierai, 'How a tiny startup became the most important hacking shop you've never heard of', *Vice*, 7 February 2018, www.vice.com/en/article/8xdayg/iphone-zero-days-inside-azimuth-security.

3   David Pegg & Sam Cutler, 'What is Pegasus Spyware and how does it hack phones?', *The Guardian*, 19 July 2021.

4   See Azimuth Security, 2023, www.azimuthsecurity.com.

5   'Risky Biz Feature Interview: Mark Dowd on the 0day market and future of exceptional access', podcast, *Risky Biz*, 19 October 2021, https://risky.biz/HF13.

6   CNN, 'San Bernardino Shooting', 2016, https://edition.cnn.com/specials/san-bernardino-shooting.

7   Danny Yadron, Spencer Ackerman & Sam Thielman, 'Inside the FBI's encryption battle with Apple', *The Guardian*, 18 February 2016, www.theguardian.com/technology/2016/feb/17/inside-the-fbis-encryption-battle-with-apple.

8   Ibid.

9   Ellen Nakashima & Reed Albergotti, 'The FBI wanted to unlock the San Bernardino shooter's iPhone. It turned to a little-known Australian firm', *The Washington Post*, 14 April 2021, https://www.washingtonpost.com/technology/2021/04/14/azimuth-san-bernardino-apple-iphone-fbi/

10 'Risky Biz Feature Interview: Mark Dowd on the 0day market and future of exceptional access', podcast, *Risky Biz*, 19 October 2021, https://risky.biz/HF13.

11 Ibid.

12 Paul Schwartz & Karl-Nikolaus Peifer, 'Transatlantic data privacy law', *Georgetown Law Journal*, vol. 106, 2017, p. 115.

13 Ewen Macaskill & Gabriel Dance, 'NSA files decoded', *The Guardian*, 1 November 2013, www.theguardian.com/world/interactive/2013/nov/01/snowden-nsa-files-surveillance-revelations-decoded.

14 Rick Sarre, 'Metadata retention as a means of combatting terrorism and organised crime: A perspective from Australia', *Asian Journal of Criminology*, vol. 12, 2017, pp. 167–79.

15 *Telecommunications (Interception and Access) Amendment (Data Retention) Act 2015* (Cth).

16 Prime Minister Tony Abbott, cited in Michelle Grattan, '$131 million for companies' metadata retention in budget boost to counter terrorism', *The Conversation*, 12 May 2015, https://theconversation.com/131-million-for-companies-metadata-retention-in-budget-boost-to-counter-terrorism-41637

17 Yolanda Redrup, 'Experts demand increased transparency in metadata surveillance laws', *Australian Financial Review*, 23 July 2019.

18 US Senate Committee on the Judiciary, *Graham, Cotton, Blackburn Introduce Balanced Solution to Bolster National Security, End Use of Warrant-Proof Encryption that Shields Criminal Activity*, 23 June 2020, www.judiciary.senate.gov/press/rep/releases/graham-cotton-blackburn-introduce-balanced-solution-to-bolster-national-security-end-use-of-warrant-proof-encryption-that-shields-criminal-activity.

19 Lindsay Clarke, 'Wrong time to weaken encryption, UK IT Chartered Institute tells government', *The Register*, 18 April 2023, www.theregister.com/2023/04/18/wrong_time_to_weaken_encryption.

20 *Telecommunications and Other Legislation Amendment (Assistance and Access) Act 2018* (Cth).

21 Marcus Smith & Gregor Urbas, *Technology Law: Australian and International Perspectives*, Cambridge University Press, 2021.

22 Ibid.

23 Francis Galbally, *Questions on Notice from Senetas Corporation*, Parliamentary Joint Committee on Intelligence and Security, Review of the Telecommunications and Other Legislation Amendment (Assistance and Access) Bill 2018, Parliament of Australia, 2018.

24 Australian Federal Police, 'AFP-led Operation Ironside smashes organised crime', 8 June 2021, www.afp.gov.au/news-media/media-releases/afp-led-operation-ironside-smashes-organised-crime.

6. Face Value

1 Max Raskin, 'Interview with Hoan Ton-That', 15 October 2021, www.maxraskin.com/interviews/hoan-ton-that.

2 Marcus Smith, Monique Mann & Gregor Urbas, *Biometrics, Crime and Security*, Routledge, 2018.

3 Ibid.

4 Josh Taylor, 'Why is Facebook shutting down its facial recognition system

and deleting "faceprints"?', *The Guardian*, 3 November 2021, www.theguardian.com/technology/2021/nov/03/why-is-facebook-shutting-down-its-facial-recognition-system-and-deleting-faceprints.

5   Clearview AI, 2023, www.clearview.ai.

6   Kashmir Hill, 'The secretive company that might end privacy as we know it', *The New York Times*, 18 January 2020, www.nytimes.com/2020/01/18/technology/clearview-privacy-facial-recognition.html.

7   Clearview AI, 2023, www.clearview.ai.

8   'Clearview AI agrees to restrict use of face database', *The Guardian*, 10 May 2022, www.theguardian.com/us-news/2022/may/09/clearview-chicago-settlement-aclu.

9   Australian Information and Privacy Commissioner, 'Clearview AI breached Australians' privacy', 3 November 2021, www.oaic.gov.au/newsroom/clearview-ai-breached-australians-privacy.

10 Ibid.

11 Marcus Smith, Monique Mann & Gregor Urbas, *Biometrics, Crime and Security*, Routledge, 2018.

12 Marcus Smith & Seumas Miller, *Biometric Identification, Law and Ethics*, Springer, 2021.

13 Australian Human Rights Commission, *Facial Recognition and Biometric Tech*, 2023, https://tech.humanrights.gov.au/artificial-intelligence/facial-recognition-biometric-tech.

7. Gene Pool

1   'Anne Wojcicki', *Forbes*, 2022, www.forbes.com/profile/anne-wojcicki.

2   23andMe, 2023, www.23andme.com/en-int.

3   A related term you're likely familiar with, genetics, refers to the study of single genes and how traits are passed on to later generations. See National Human Genome Research Institute, *A Brief Guide to Genomics*, 2019.

4   Kristen Brown, 'All those 23andMe spit tests were part of a bigger plan', *Bloomberg*, 4 November 2021, www.bloomberg.com/news/features/2021-11-04/23andme-to-use-dna-tests-to-make-cancer-drugs.

5   Myriad Genetics, 2023, www.myriad.com.

6   *Association for Molecular Pathology v. Myriad Genetics, Inc.,* (133 S. Ct. 2107) (2013), 2111. Myriad Genetics also sought to patent BRCA1 in Australia, which resulted in extensive litigation there too. It was eventually heard by the High Court in the case *D'Arcy v. Myriad Genetics Inc.*, which reached a similar conclusion as the US Supreme Court, holding that the invention was not 'a manner of manufacture' within the meaning of the *Patents Act 1990* (Cth).

7   Federal Bureau of Investigation, *The FBI Story 2016*, Department of Justice, 2017, pp. 62–66.

8   Joseph Zabel, 'The killer inside us: Law, ethics, and the forensic use of family genetics', *Berkeley Journal of Criminal Law*, vol. 24, 2019, pp. 47–100.

9   Marcus Smith & Seumas Miller, 'A principled approach to cross sector genomic data access', *Bioethics*, vol. 35, 2021, pp. 779–86.

10   Marcus Smith, *DNA Evidence in the Australian Legal System*, LexisNexis, 2016.

11   Federal Bureau of Investigation, 'NDIS Statistics', www.fbi.gov/services/laboratory/biometric-analysis/codis/ndis-statistics. United Kingdom Government, *National DNA Database Statistics*, www.gov.uk/government/statistics/national-dna-database-statistics.

12   [2008] ECHR 1581.

13   Marcus Smith & Seumas Miller, 'A principled approach to cross sector genomic data access', *Bioethics*, vol. 35, 2021, pp. 779–86.

14   Antonio Regalado, 'More than 26 million people have taken an at-home ancestry test', *MIT Technology Review*, 11 February 2019.

15   Nathan Scudder et al., 'Operationalising forensic genetic genealogy in an Australian context', *Forensic Science International*, vol. 316, 2020, pp. 1–8.

16   Gregory Feero et al., 'Precision medicine, genome sequencing, and improved population health', *Journal of the American Medical Association*, vol. 319, 2018, pp. 1979–80.

17   Nuffield Council on Bioethics, Horizon Scanning Workshops, 2019, https://nuffieldbioethics.org/futurework/horizon-scanning-workshops.

18   23andMe, 'Privacy policy', www.23andme.com/en-eu/legal/privacy.

8. News Business

1   Saheli Choudhury, 'Facebook cuts deal with Australia, will restore news pages in the coming days', CNBC, 2 February 2021, www.cnbc.com/2021/02/23/facebook-to-restore-news-pages-for-australian-users-in-coming-days.html.

2   Ibid.

3   Parliament of Australia, 'Hon. Josh Frydenberg', 2023, www.aph.gov.au/Senators_and_Members/Parliamentarian?MPID=FKL.

4   Ben Mezrich, *The Accidental Billionaires*, Doubleday, 2009.

5   Marcus Smith & Gregor Urbas, *Technology Law*, Cambridge University Press, 2021.

6   David Richards, 'The rise of the fifth estate', *Spectator Australia*, 18 March 2023.

7   Joshua Robertson, 'Johnny Depp's dogs: Australia's deputy PM threatens actor with "perjury" investigation', *The Guardian*, 27 June 2017.

8   Jonathan Masters, 'U.S. gun policy: Global comparisons', Council on Foreign Relations, 10 June 2022, www.cfr.org/backgrounder/us-gun-policy-global-comparisons.

9   Saheli Choudhury, 'Facebook cuts deal with Australia, will restore news pages in the coming days', CNBC, 2 February 2021, www.cnbc.com/2021/02/23/facebook-to-restore-news-pages-for-australian-users-in-coming-days.html.

10   BBC News, 'Facebook blocks Australian users from viewing or sharing news', 18 February 2021, www.bbc.com/news/world-australia-56099523.

11   Ibid.

12   Nic Fildes, 'Australian media thrives after forcing big tech to pay for content', *The Financial Times*, 10 March 2022, www.ft.com/content/80db14de-8268-4356-b7fe-a184f319f331.

13   Australian Competition and Consumer Commission, *News Media Bargaining Code*, 2021, www.accc.gov.au/by-industry/digital-platforms-and-services/news-media-bargaining-code/news-media-bargaining-code.

14   Annika Burgess, 'Meta is ending its deals to pay for Australian news content. This is how it could change your Facebook and Instagram feeds', *ABC News*, Australian Broadcasting Corporation, 2 March 2024, https://www.abc.net.au/news/2024-03-02/facebook-google-news-media-deal-media-pay-meta/103534342.

15   Anya Schiffrin, 'Australia's new soft power: Bargaining codes start to spread globally', *Tech Policy Press*, 28 April 2023.

16   Josh Taylor, 'Facebook whistleblowers allege Meta may have breached Australia's foreign interference laws', *The Guardian*, 23 May 2023.

17   In 2024, Uber agreed to pay $272 million to Australian taxi and hire car drivers in compensation for the reduced values of their licences and lost income. Jessica Riga, 'Uber will pay millions in a class action settlement. Here's what it means for the rideshare giant, competitors and consumers', *ABC News*, Australian Broadcasting Corporation, 18 March 2024, https://www.abc.net.au/news/2024-03-18/uber-class-action-settlement-from-taxi-drivers-explained/103600654.

9. Building with Blocks

1   Dan Ashmore, 'Who is Sam Bankman-Fried?', *Forbes*, 21 November 2022, www.forbes.com/advisor/investing/cryptocurrency/who-is-sam-bankman-fried.

2   Eric Rosenberg, 'Who is Sam Bankman-Fried?', *Investopedia*, 18 February 2023, www.investopedia.com/who-is-sam-bankman-fried-6830274.

3   Sam Levine, 'FTX founder Sam Bankman-Fried charged with 12 counts

in new indictment', *The Guardian*, 24 February 2023, www.theguardian.com/business/2023/feb/23/ftx-sam-bankman-fried-cryptocurrency-exchange-charges. US Department of Justice, 'Samuel Bankman-Fried Sentenced to 25 Years for His Orchestration of Multiple Fraudulent Schemes' 28 March 2024, https://www.justice.gov/opa/pr/samuel-bankman-fried-sentenced-25-years-his-orchestration-multiple-fraudulent-schemes.

4   Ibid.

5   David Gura, '2022 was the year crypto came crashing down to earth', NPR News, 29 December 2022, www.npr.org/2022/12/29/1145297807/crypto-crash-ftx-cryptocurrency-bitcoin.

6   Taylor Moffett, 'CFTC & SEC: The wild west of cryptocurrency regulation', *University of Richmond Law Review*, vol. 57, 2023, p. 713.

7   Bernard Marr, 'A short history of Bitcoin and crypto currency everyone should read', *Forbes*, 6 December 2017, www.forbes.com/sites/bernardmarr/2017/12/06/a-short-history-of-bitcoin-and-crypto-currency-everyone-should-read.

8   Ethereum, 2023, https://ethereum.org.

9   William Mougayar, *The Business Blockchain: Promise, Practice, and Application of the Next Internet Technology*, Wiley, 2016.

10 Arvin Razon, 'Liberalising blockchain: An application of the GATS Digital Trade Framework', *Melbourne Journal of International Law*, vol. 20, 2019, p. 125.

11 Gregory Ferenstein, 'Thiel Fellows program is "most misdirected piece of philanthropy", says Larry Summers', *Tech Crunch*, 11 October 2013, https://techcrunch.com/2013/10/10/thiel-fellows-program-is-most-misdirected-piece-of-philanthropy-says-larry-summers.

12 'Peter Thiel announces 2014 class of Thiel Fellows', *Businesswire*, 5 June 2014, www.businesswire.com/news/home/20140605005295/en/Peter-Thiel-Announces-2014-Class-of-Thiel-Fellows.

13 Reserve Bank of Australia, *Cryptocurrencies*, 2020, www.rba.gov.au/education/resources/explainers/cryptocurrencies.html.

14 'Former Mt. Gox Bitcoin exchange boss pleads not guilty', BBC News, 11 July 2017, www.bbc.com/news/technology-40561420.

15 Marcus Smith & Gregor Urbas, *Technology Law: Australian and International Perspectives*, Cambridge University Press, 2021.

16 Marcus Smith, 'A modern approach to regulation: Integrating law, system architecture and blockchain technology in Australia', *Australian Business Law Review*, vol. 48, 2020, pp. 460–66.

17 Ibid.

18 Raja Koduri, 'Powering the metaverse', *Intel Newsroom*, 4 December 2021, www.intel.com/content/www/us/en/newsroom/opinion/powering-metaverse.html.

19 Kalhan Rosenblatt, 'Iconic "doge" meme NFT breaks record, selling for $4 million', NBC News, 12 June 2021, www.nbcnews.com/pop-culture/pop-culture-news/iconic-doge-meme-nft-breaks-records-selling-roughly-4-million-n1270161.

20 Marcus Smith & Gregor Urbas, *Technology Law: Australian and International Perspectives*, Cambridge University Press, 2021.

21 Ibid.

22 Blockchain-based Service Network, 'Introductory White Paper', 2020, https://bsnbase.io/static/tmpFile/BSNIntroductionWhitepaper.pdf.

23 Marcus Smith & Milind Tiwari, 'The implications of national blockchain infrastructure for financial crime', *Journal of Financial Crime*, 16 June 2023.

24 Michael Sung, 'China's national blockchain will change the world', 24 April 2020, www.coindesk.com/policy/2020/04/24/chinas-national-blockchain-will-change-the-world.

25 Ibid.

26 Marcus Smith, 'A modern approach to regulation: Integrating law, system architecture and blockchain technology in Australia', *Australian Business Law Review*, vol. 48, 2020, pp. 460–66.

10. Continental Style

1 Arjun Kharpal, 'Facebook brings back its controversial facial recognition feature to Europe after closing it in 2012', CNBC News, 18 April 2018, www.cnbc.com/2018/04/18/facebook-brings-back-facial-recognition-to-europe-after-closing-it-in-2012.html.

2 Jennifer Bryant, 'Facebook to close its facial recognition system, but will it start a paradigm shift?', International Association of Privacy Professionals, 3 November 2021, https://iapp.org/news/a/facebook-to-close-its-facial-recognition-system-but-will-it-start-a-paradigm-shift.

3 In 2019, facial recognition was one of the issues cited as part of the US' Federal Trade Commission's US$5 billion privacy settlement with Facebook. Facebook paid a US$650 million class-action settlement relating to 1.6 million users in the state of Illinois, on the basis it was collecting and storing individuals' face scans without notice or consent, according to legislation in that state.

4 Hanna Ziady, 'Meta slapped with record $1.3 billion EU fine over data privacy', CNN Business, 22 May 2023, https://edition.cnn.com/2023/05/22/tech/meta-facebook-data-privacy-eu-fine/index.html.

5 Ibid.

6 Ibid.

7 Bobby Allyn, 'Why Margrethe Vestager is Silicon Valley's most prominent antagonist', NPR News, 15 December 2022, www.npr.

org/2022/12/15/1143191951/encore-why-margrethe-vestager-is-silicon-valley-s-most-prominent-antagonist.

8   Ibid.

9   'Biden signs order to implement EU–US data privacy framework', Reuters, 7 October 2022, https://edition.cnn.com/2022/10/07/tech/biden-eu-data-privacy-order/index.html.

10   *Google Spain SL v. AEPD & Mario Costeja Gonzalez*, C-131/12, 13 May 2014.

11   Alan Travis & Charles Arthur, 'EU court backs "right to be forgotten": Google must amend results on request', *The Guardian*, 13 May 2014, www.theguardian.com/technology/2014/may/13/right-to-be-forgotten-eu-court-google-search-results.

12   Ibid.

13   *Google Spain SL v. AEPD & Mario Costeja Gonzalez*, C-131/12, 13 May 2014.

14   Marcus Smith & Gregor Urbas, *Technology Law: Australian and International Perspectives*, Cambridge University Press, 2021.

15   *Google v. Commission Nationale de l'informatique et des libertes (CNIL)*, EUR-Lex CELEX, No. 62017CJ0507, 24 September 2019.

16   Ibid.

17   Article 17.

18   Articles 6, 17, 16, 20, 22 and 34.

19   Article 32.

20   Stefan Larsson, 'Metaphors, law and digital phenomena: The Swedish Pirate Bay court case', *International Journal of Law and Information Technology*, vol. 21, 2013, pp. 354, 358–59.

21   *Stichting Brein v. Ziggo,* Case C-610/15.

22   Alex Hern, 'European Court of Justice rules Pirate Bay is infringing copyright', *The Guardian*, 15 June 2017, www.theguardian.com/technology/2017/jun/15/pirate-bay-european-court-of-justice-rules-infringing-copyright-torrent-sites.

23   Gregor Urbas, 'Public enforcement of intellectual property rights', *Trends and Issues in Crime and Criminal Justice*, no. 177, 2000.

24   Marcus Smith & Gregor Urbas, *Technology Law: Australian and International Perspectives*, Cambridge University Press, 2021.

25   Stefan Larsson, 'Metaphors, law and digital phenomena: The Swedish Pirate Bay court case', *International Journal of Law and Information Technology*, vol. 21, 2013, pp. 354, 358.

26   See, for example, the *Digital Millennium Copyright Act 1998* (US).

27   United States Copyright Office, *The Digital Millennium Copyright Act*, www.copyright.gov/dmca.

28   *C682/18 Peterson v. Google LLC et al.* and *C683/18 Elsevier Inc v. Cyando AG.*

29   Brooks Barnes, 'TV and movie actors vote for biggest walkout in

four decades', *The New York Times*, 13 July 2023, www.nytimes.com/live/2023/07/13/business/actors-strike-sag.

30 Articles 2, 5, 10, 11 and 14.

31 *Ahmet Yildirim v. Turkey*, no 3111/10, 18 December 2012, [54].

32 Yeşil Deniz, *Online Freedoms and the European Court of Human Rights: A Path Forward for Turkey?*, Centre for Economics and Foreign Policy Studies, 2018.

33 *Big Brother Watch and Others v. the United Kingdom,* App. Nos. 58170/13, 62322/14, 24960/15, 25 May 2021.

34 Ailidh Callander & Scarlet Kim, 'European court ruling could recognize mass surveillance violates human rights', American Civil Liberties Union, 2017.

35 Monika Zalnieriute, 'Big Brother Watch and Others v. the United Kingdom', American Journal of International Law, vol. 116, 2022, pp. 585–92.

36 Digital Services Act Regulation (EU) 2022/2065; Digital Markets Act (DMA) Regulation (EU) 2022/1925.

37 Alex Engler, 'Platform data access is a lynchpin of the EU's Digital Services Act', Brookings Institute, 15 January 2021, www.brookings.edu/blog/techtank/2021/01/15/platform-data-access-is-a-lynchpin-of-the-eus-digital-services-act.

38 'The U.S. could learn from Europe's online speech rule', *The Washington Post*, 29 January 2022, www.washingtonpost.com/opinions/2022/01/29/us-could-learn-europes-online-speech-rules.

39 European Commission, *Impact assessment of the Digital Markets Act 2020*, https://digital-strategy.ec.europa.eu/en/library/impact-assessment-digital-markets-act.

40 Adi Robertson, 'How the EU is fighting tech giants with Margrethe Vestager', *The Verge*, 18 March 2022, www.theverge.com/22981261/margrethe-vestager-decoder-antitrust-eu-apple-facebook-google-jedi-blue.

41 European Union, *Regulatory Framework Proposal on Artificial Intelligence*, 2022, https://digital-strategy.ec.europa.eu/en/policies/regulatory-framework-ain.

42 Ibid.

43 'What is the European Union AI Act?', Reuters, 22 March 2023, www.reuters.com/technology/what-is-european-union-ai-act-2023-03-22.

11. Techno 2.0

1 Techno Station, 'A short history of techno in Berlin', 2023, www.technostation.tv/short-history-of-techno-in-berlin.

2 Beate Peter, 'Berlin Wall: How techno music united Germany on the dance floor', *The Conversation*, 8 November 2019, https://theconversation.

com/berlin-wall-how-techno-music-united-germany-on-the-dance-floor-125280.

3   Gilberto Gerra et al., 'Neuroendocrine responses of healthy volunteers to "techno-music": Relationships with personality traits and emotional state', *International Journal of Psychophysiology*, vol. 28, 1998, pp. 99–111.

4   Marcus Smith & Seumas Miller, 'Technology, institutions and regulation: Towards a normative theory', *AI & Society*, https://link.springer.com/article/10.1007/s00146-023-01803-0.

5   David Johnson & David Post, 'Law and borders: The rise of law in cyberspace', *Stanford Law Review*, vol. 48, 1996, pp. 1367, 1402.

6   '[T]he set of rules for information flows imposed by technology and communication networks form a "Lex Informatica" that policymakers must understand, consciously recognize, and encourage': Joel Reidenberg, 'Lex informatica: The formulation of information policy rules through technology', *Texas Law Review*, vol. 76, 1998, p. 553.

7   Lawrence Lessig, 'The law of the horse: What cyberlaw might teach', *Harvard Law Review*, vol. 113, 1991, pp. 501, 512.

8   Lessig developed the phrase 'code is law' to explain the above idea, playing on the use of the word 'code' to refer to the text of a computer program as well as legislative provisions. He has also argued for the liberalisation of technology policy, supporting open-source software and the 'free culture' movement, which promotes the free exchange of creative works and access to knowledge. Lessig founded the Creative Commons movement in 2001, known for expanding the availability of educational content around the world, making it easier for copyright owners and authors to waive rights and share content.

9   Lawrence Lessig, *Code and Other Laws of Cyberspace*, Basic Books, 1999, p. 96.

10 Antonio Pequeno, 'OpenAI CEO Sam Altman urges greater AI regulation – including new federal agency – at historic congressional hearing', *Forbes*, 16 May 2023, www.forbes.com/sites/antoniopequenoiv/2023/05/16/openai-ceo-sam-altman-urges-greater-ai-regulation-including-new-federal-agency-at-historic-congressional-hearing.

11 Joshua Meltzer, 'The US government should regulate AI if it wants to lead on international AI governance', Brookings Institute, 22 May 2023, www.brookings.edu/blog/up-front/2023/05/22/the-us-government-should-regulate-ai.

12 Ibid.

13 Ibid.

Acknowledgements

I am grateful to University of Queensland Press, Madonna Duffy, Jacqueline Blanchard, Julian Welch, Gregor Urbas, Mark Nolan and Seumas Miller for their assistance in the production and publication of this book, and their support of my work.